ADVENTURE TALES OF THE
CONSTITUTION OF THE UNITED STATES

From The Book

ADVENTURE TALES OF AMERICA
An Illustrated History Of The United States, 1492-1877

Jody Potts, Ph.D.

ILLUSTRATORS

Foy Lisenby, Ph.D.
Jerry D. Poole, Ph.D.

Signal Media Publishers

Dallas, Texas

AUTHOR

Jody Potts, a native Texan, has taught graduate courses in American intellectual, cultural, and political history at Southern Methodist University in Dallas for two decades and served as visiting professor at Alaska Pacific University for three summers. In SMU's Master of Liberal Arts Program she currently teaches a course on the history of American ideas, **Ideas that Shaped the American Character,** and a course she originated, **The Lively Mind: Creative and Critical Thinking Using Both Sides of the Brain.** She holds a B.S. degree in education from Baylor University, an M.A. degree in history from Southern Methodist University, and a Ph.D. degree in history from the University of North Texas.

A specialist in left and right brain learning techniques, Dr. Potts pioneered the integration of these techniques with the teaching and writing of history. In 1993 she wrote *Adventure Tales of America: An Illustrated History of the United States, 1492-1877,* an innovative book that accelerates learning by simultaneously giving information to the left brain through words, analysis, and structure and the right brain through pictures, humor, and drama. *Adventure Tales of America,* now a multimedia program, has raised state history scores throughout the country, as much as eighteen percent with grade-level students and 115 percent with at-risk students. In 2000 she wrote *Adventure Tales of Benjamin Banneker.* Both *Adventure Tales* books were published by Signal Media Publishers.

Adventure Tales of the Constitution of the United States is an expansion of the story that appears in *Adventure Tales of America: An Illustrated History of the United States, 1492-1877* (shown on opposite page).

In 1984 Dr. Potts founded **The Lively Mind,** a national consulting firm offering seminars in left and right brain learning techniques for students, faculties, and administrators. Participating groups have included public schools nationwide, state social studies councils, the Council for Support and Advancement of Education, and the University of Texas at Austin senior faculty. She serves on North Texas University's Department of History Advisory Board and was recently selected as an outstanding alumna of the University. She is a member of the Presidents' Circle of the National Academy of Sciences.

ILLUSTRATORS

Foy Lisenby, a specialist in American social and cultural history and a gifted cartoonist, served fifteen years as chairman of the University of Central Arkansas History Department. He has published numerous articles and, in 1996, a biography of Charles Hillman Brough.

Jerry D. Poole served as professor of art at the University of Central Arkansas until 1989, chairing the Art Department for seventeen years. He is an accomplished silhouette artist and specializes in watercolor painting.

PUBLISHER

Copyright © 2001 by Signal Media Publishers
SignalMedia Publishers acknowledges the use of some of its previously copyrighted materials from *Adventure Tales of America: An Illustrated History of the United States, 1492-1877.*

Signal Media Publishers specializes in innovative learning materials.
To preview and order visit www.adventuretales.com or call 1-800-494-2445.

ISBN: 1-887337-08-3   Library of Congress PCN Number: 2001118490   Printed in the United States of America   10 9 8 7 6 5 4 3 2 1

Adventure Tales of America

Multimedia U.S. History Program, 1492-1877

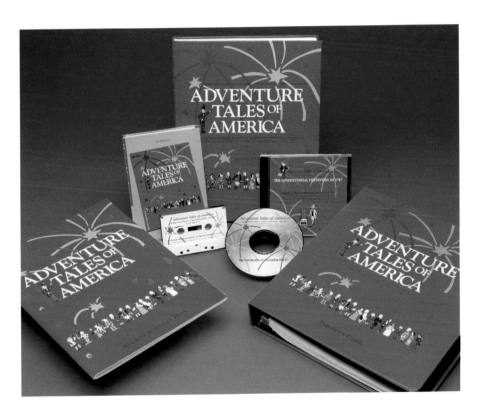

Get set for an adventure in learning!

From exploration of the New World to the Civil War and Reconstruction, America's story unfolds with high drama – absorbing, entertaining, and enlightening.

For more information go to

www.adventuretales.com

or call Signal Media Publishers 1-800-494-2445.

ACKNOWLEDGMENTS

James Madison

"[Of] The affairs of the United States, he perhaps has the most correct knowledge...of any Man in the Union."
– William L. Pierce, Convention Delegate 1787

Independence Hall
Philadelphia, Pennsylvania

"You give me too much credit," said James Madison when he was called the Father of the Constitution. Despite Madison's modesty, historians continue to honor him with this title because of his extraordinary contributions to the Constitution of the United States.

James Madison

• analyzed ancient and modern governments in preparation for the Federal Convention (later called the Constitutional Convention)

• wrote a detailed plan for the Constitution, most of which was adopted

• gave Americans a ring-side seat at the Convention through the notes he took of the delegates' debates

• published 29 newspaper essays supporting ratification of the Constitution. (Later these became part of *The Federalist Papers*.)

Credit must go to James Madison for this book, ***Adventure Tales of the Constitution of the United States,*** for it is based on his *Notes of Debates in the Federal Convention of 1787.* I hope all who read *Adventure Tales* will be inspired to read Madison's *Notes of Debates,* the primary document for understanding the Constitution of the United States.

Americans are indebted to the National Park Service for preserving Independence Hall, site of the Constitutional Convention. You can visit Independence Hall, our country's birthplace, and see for yourself where Madison, Washington, Franklin, Hamilton, and others created the self-government we enjoy today. What an adventure!

Jody Potts

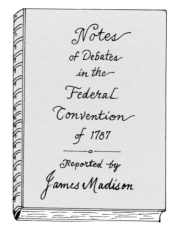

Madison's notes were published in 1840, four years after his death.

Assembly Room
Independence Hall

"I chose a seat in front of the presiding member, with the other members on my right and left hand."
– James Madison

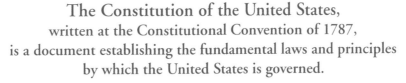

1607   1787   2010

"The most wonderful work ever struck off at a given time by the brain and purpose of man."

—William E. Gladstone

The Constitution of the United States of America

Preamble

We the People of the United States,
in Order to form a more perfect Union,
establish Justice,
ensure domestic Tranquillity,
provide for the common defense,
promote the general Welfare, and
secure the Blessings of Liberty to ourselves and our Posterity,
do ordain and establish this
Constitution for the United States of America.

The Constitution of the United States,
written at the Constitutional Convention of 1787,
is a document establishing the fundamental laws and principles
by which the United States is governed.

It sets forth a structure of self-government based on the consent of the governed.
It is the highest law of the land, and as such it protects our rights and freedoms.
It is short—containing a preamble, or introduction, seven articles, and
27 amendments (including the first ten, called the Bill of Rights).

It was written not by central or state governments
but, as the preamble states, by
"We the people of the United States."

THE UNITED STATES OF AMERICA
"LAND OF THE FREE AND HOME OF THE BRAVE"

THE STAR-SPANGLED BANNER

Oh, say can you see by the dawn's early light
What so proudly we hailed at the twilight's last gleaming,
Whose broad stripes and bright stars through the perilous fight
O'er the ramparts we watched were so gallantly streaming?
And the rockets' red glare, the bombs bursting in air,
Gave proof through the night that our flag was still there.
Oh, say does that star-spangled banner yet wave
O'er the land of the free and the home of the brave?

Written by Francis Scott Key in 1814;
adopted as the United States' national anthem in 1931

THE PLEDGE OF ALLEGIANCE

I pledge allegiance to the flag
of the United States of America
and to the republic for which it stands,
one nation under God, indivisible,
with liberty and justice for all.

Written by Francis Bellamy in 1882;
adopted as the United States' national pledge in 1942

CONTENTS

"TO FORM A MORE PERFECT UNION"

Why did
"We the people of the United States"
write a Constitution?

The answer is in the preamble of the Constitution:
**"to form a more perfect Union...
and secure the Blessings of Liberty
to ourselves and our Posterity...."**
And this answer leads to exciting adventure tales.

The adventure tales of the Constitution of the United States
did not begin in 1787, the year it was written.
They began long before.

Abraham Lincoln explained it this way in 1861:

"The Union is much older than the Constitution.
It was formed, in fact, by the Articles of Association in 1774.
It was matured and continued by the Declaration of Independence in 1776.
It was further matured, and the faith of all the then thirteen States expressedly
plighted and engaged that it should be perpetual, by the Articles of Confederation of 1778.
And finally, in 1787, one of the declared objects for ordaining and establishing the Constitution, was
"to form a more perfect union."

—President Abraham Lincoln
First Inaugural Address, 1861

Now, you can explore for yourself what happened...

1492

1788

COLONIZATION: AN OVERVIEW

In 1607 England founded the first of thirteen colonies on North America's East Coast and successfully ruled them for 169 years.*

Other nationalities helped settle the colonies, but the population, language, laws, and culture remained predominantly British. Most colonists were proud to be subjects of the mighty British empire.

Then—in 1776 the colonies broke free of their mother country and became the United States of America.

WHY?

It all started with the French and Indian War. In 1763 the British defeated the French and gained new land in North America—and then asked, "Why don't we tax the colonists to help pay for the war?" And then one thing led to another.

THE THIRTEEN ORIGINAL COLONIES

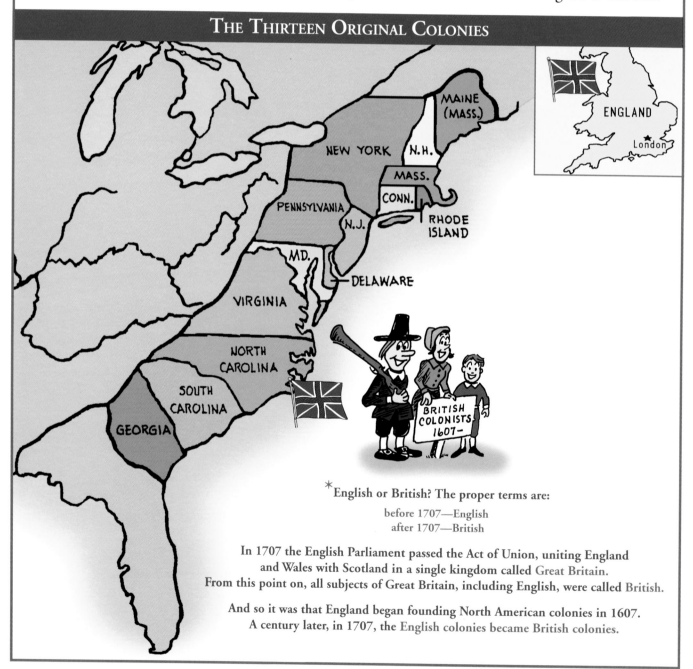

*English or British? The proper terms are:

before 1707—English
after 1707—British

In 1707 the English Parliament passed the Act of Union, uniting England and Wales with Scotland in a single kingdom called Great Britain. From this point on, all subjects of Great Britain, including English, were called British.

And so it was that England began founding North American colonies in 1607. A century later, in 1707, the English colonies became British colonies.

"I think the Parliament of Great Britain hath no more right to put their hands into my pocket, without my consent, than I have to put my hands into yours for money...."—George Washington

1763

1787

1754-1763: THE FRENCH AND INDIAN WAR CHANGED EVERYTHING.

FRENCH AND INDIAN WAR 1754-1763

Before 1763 Great Britain paid little attention to her colonies, 3,000 miles distant. **After 1763** victorious Great Britain tightened control of her vast North American empire (almost doubled in size with land won from France). King George III and the British Parliament took action that seemed fair to them, unfair to the colonists—and led directly to the American Revolution. Parliament's most provocative action? TAXATION WITHOUT REPRESENTATION.

1776-83: DECLARATION OF INDEPENDENCE AND AMERICAN REVOLUTION

DECLARATION OF INDEPENDENCE 1776

In 1776 the thirteen American colonies declared their independence from Great Britain and formed thirteen independent state governments. Led by General George Washington, the Americans fought a seven-year revolutionary war, finally winning independence in 1783 and gaining land stretching west to the Mississippi River.

HOW WOULD THE AMERICANS GOVERN THEMSELVES?

AMERICAN REVOLUTION 1776 – 1783

1781-88: ARTICLES OF CONFEDERATION

PENNSYLVANIA

CONFEDERATION PERIOD 13 SOVEREIGN STATES 1781-1788

At first the Americans had no intention of forming a national government, afraid it might threaten individual liberty. Instead, in 1781, they adopted the Articles of Confederation, creating a one-branch central government. They agreed that each state would keep its sovereignty and independence, while cooperating with the others in a Confederation—a "perpetual League of Friendship."

EACH STATE WAS LIKE A SEPARATE COUNTRY.

JUDICIAL (COURTS)   LEGISLATIVE (CONGRESS)   EXECUTIVE (PRESIDENT)

1787: CONFEDERATION PROBLEMS TRIGGER THE CONSTITUTIONAL CONVENTION.

The Confederation was weak and in debt because Congress lacked two powers: 1) taxation, and 2) trade regulation. Alexander Hamilton, James Madison, and others urged Congress to call a Convention of all thirteen states to revise the Articles. The Convention instead overthrew the Articles, based on state sovereignty, and created the Constitution of the United States, based on national sovereignty.

HOW DID THE CONFEDERATION LEAD TO THE CONVENTION?

THE U.S. CONSTITUTION (RATIFIED 1788)

THE BIG QUESTION: WHO WILL BE IN CHARGE?

INDEPENDENCE BROUGHT PROBLEMS! WHO WOULD BE IN CHARGE? NOT A KING—THAT'S FOR SURE!

YEAH, WHAT KIND OF GOVERNMENT WOULD THE FREEDOM-LOVING AMERICANS CREATE TO BALANCE LIBERTY WITH ENOUGH AUTHORITY TO GET THINGS DONE FOR THE COMMON GOOD? IT TOOK A FEW YEARS OF TRIAL AND ERROR TO FIND THE RIGHT BALANCE.

I SEE. THE STATES WERE SORT OF LIKE 13 LITTLE COUNTRIES BELONGING TO THE UNITED NATIONS!

AT FIRST THE AMERICANS HAD NO INTENTION OF FORMING A NATIONAL GOVERNMENT—AFRAID IT MIGHT LIMIT THEIR LIBERTIES! SO IN 1781, THEY ADOPTED THE ARTICLES OF CONFEDERATION, AGREEING THAT EACH STATE WOULD KEEP IT'S "SOVEREIGNTY (SUPREME POWER), FREEDOM AND INDEPENDENCE," WHILE COOPERATING WITH THE OTHERS IN A CONFEDERATION—"A PERPETUAL LEAGUE OF FRIENDSHIP."

YES, BUT BY 1787 THERE WERE SUCH PROBLEMS THAT SOME PEOPLE WERE READY FOR A NATIONAL GOVERNMENT.

WELL, SEE FOR YOURSELF WHAT HAPPENED...

SHIFTING BALANCE OF POWER: AN OVERVIEW

MONARCHY   1607–1776
BRITISH CONSTITUTION (UNWRITTEN)

CONFEDERATION   1781–1788
ARTICLES OF CONFEDERATION

REPUBLIC   1788
U.S. CONSTITUTION

A MORE PERFECT UNION

NATIONAL SOVEREIGNTY • • • STATES RIGHTS

NATIONAL GOVT.   STATES

"The Stile of this confederacy shall be 'The United States of America.'"

—Articles of Confederation, Article I,
Ratified March 1, 1781

ARTICLES OF CONFEDERATION
The United States' first Constitution, 1781-88

On June 7, 1776, Richard Henry Lee, Virginia delegate to the Continental Congress, proposed that the "United Colonies are, and of right ought to be, free and independent states," and that "a plan of confederation be prepared and transmitted to the respective colonies for their consideration and approbation."

A plan called the Articles of Confederation was adopted by Congress in 1777 and ratified by 12 of the 13 states by 1779. Maryland withheld ratification until states with claims to western lands ceded those lands to Congress "for the good of the whole." By 1781 all states with land claims had agreed to cede them, and on March 1, Maryland ratified the Articles.

On March 1, 1781, the Articles of Confederation became the law of the land—and remained so until replaced in 1788 by the Constitution of the United States.

ARTICLES OF CONFEDERATION: 13 SOVEREIGN STATES

sovereign—supreme power; independent

THE CONFEDERATION GOVERNMENT UNDER THE ARTICLES OF CONFEDERATION, 1781-88

The Confederation Government—despite certain limitations—successfully fought the American Revolution, won independence, and negotiated a remarkably favorable peace treaty.

YOU WOULDN'T HAVE RECOGNIZED THE CONFEDERATION GOVERNMENT OF 1781-1788. IT HAD ONLY ONE BRANCH—THE LEGISLATIVE, CALLED CONGRESS.

JUDICIAL (COURTS)   LEGISLATIVE (CONGRESS)   EXECUTIVE (PRESIDENT)

The single-house Congress was composed of two-to-seven delegates from each state, who voted as a unit.

No matter how large a state in population, it had only one vote in Congress.

Votes of two-thirds of the states were required to pass laws.

Amendments to the Articles required a unanimous vote. This made it hard to change the Articles of Confederation.

CONGRESS, DESIGNED TO BE WEAK, HAD FEW POWERS.

Congress could:

1. Declare war
2. Make treaties
3. Manage Indian affairs
4. Maintain an army and navy
5. Coin and borrow money
6. Regulate weights and measures
7. Establish a postal service

CONGRESS WAS CRIPPLED BECAUSE IT HAD NO POWER TO RAISE TAXES OR REGULATE TRADE.

IT'S THE GOLDEN RULE: "HE WHO HAS THE GOLD MAKES THE RULES."

CAN YOU FIGURE OUT TWO BIG POWERS CONGRESS LACKED?

STATE POWERS

The thirteen sovereign states followed this golden rule. Each controlled its own purse strings, holding the power to:

1. tax

2. regulate trade.

STATE CONSTITUTIONS

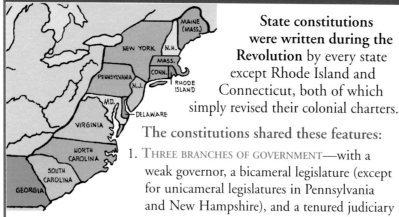

State constitutions were written during the Revolution by every state except Rhode Island and Connecticut, both of which simply revised their colonial charters.

The constitutions shared these features:

1. THREE BRANCHES OF GOVERNMENT—with a weak governor, a bicameral legislature (except for unicameral legislatures in Pennsylvania and New Hampshire), and a tenured judiciary

2. PROPERTY QUALIFICATIONS FOR VOTING AND HOLDING OFFICE

3. BILLS OF RIGHTS to guarantee personal liberty. Virginia's Bill of Rights, called the Declaration of Rights, was written in June 1776 by George Mason. It became a model for those of other states and for the United States Bill of Rights.

LAND GAINED AFTER THE REVOLUTION

In the 1783 Treaty of Paris, Britain ceded to the United States land extending west to the Mississippi River. How would the new western territory be settled, organized, and governed?

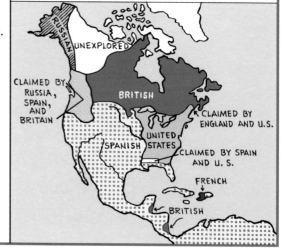

Democratic Achievements of the Confederation

In 1784 Thomas Jefferson, serving in the Confederation Congress, created a plan of government for organizing western lands into states on an equal basis with the original thirteen. His plan—including grid surveys, public education, prohibition of slavery, religious freedom, and self-government—was incorporated in the Land Ordinance of 1785 and Northwest Ordinance of 1787.

Land Ordinance of 1785—Jefferson's Plan for Surveying and Selling Western Lands

The Northwest Territory (and later, other territories) would be surveyed and divided into townships, each six miles square. The townships would be subdivided into 36 sections, one mile square (640 acres).

OH BOY! HERE COME THE SETTLERS!

I THINK THEY'RE GOING TO SURVEY THIS TERRITORY AND GOVERN US, TOO.

WHOOPEE

NORTHWEST TERRITORY

Sections of land would be sold at public auction for a minimum of $1.00 per acre. Section 16 of each town would be used to support public education—a priceless gift.

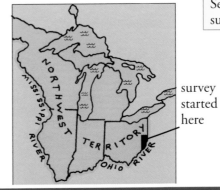

survey started here

6 mile square township

6	5	4	3	2	1
7	8	9	10	11	12
18	17	16	15	14	13
19	20	21	22	23	24
30	29	28	27	26	25
31	32	33	34	35	36

One mile square section, 640 acres

Northwest Ordinance of 1787—Republican Statehood for the New Territories

♦ **Allowed the Northwest Territory to divide into three to five territories**—each with self-government and a bill of rights that included religious freedom.

♦ **Prohibited slavery** in the Northwest Territory—based on Thomas Jefferson's 1784 proposal.

Jefferson had proposed prohibiting slavery in ALL future states after 1800, but this clause lost by <u>one</u> vote in 1784. He lamented: "The voice of a single individual would have prevented this abominable crime from spreading itself over the new country."

> **TERRITORIAL GOVERNMENT WOULD DEVELOP IN THREE STAGES:**
> (This plan also applied to subsequent territories.)
> 1. a **Congressionally appointed governor** and 3 judges at the first stage,
> 2. an **elected legislature** and a non-voting delegate to Congress when the population reached 5,000 free, white males,
> 3. a **state constitution** and admission to statehood when the above population reached 60,000.

The Northwest Ordinance set an important land policy by taking in new western lands as equal states rather than subordinate colonies, a democratic policy rare in history.

Expansion of Freedoms in the States

♦ **Anglican Church disestablished, 1776-1790.**

♦ **Feudal property laws abolished.**

1) PRIMOGENITURE: right of the oldest son to property inheritance
2) ENTAIL: land inheritance restricted to descendents of original owner

♦ **Slavery abolished in northern states, 1777-1804.**

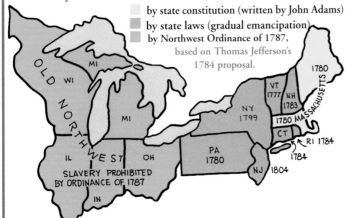

by state constitution (written by John Adams)
by state laws (gradual emancipation)
by Northwest Ordinance of 1787, based on Thomas Jefferson's 1784 proposal.

OLD NORTHWEST

MI, WI, MI, IL, OH, IN — SLAVERY PROHIBITED BY ORDINANCE OF 1787

VT 1777, NH 1783, NY 1799, MASSACHUSETTS 1780, CT, RI 1784, PA 1780, NJ 1804, 1780, 1784

Virginia Statute For Religious Freedom

Thomas Jefferson, after writing the Declaration of Independence in 1776, returned home to Virginia. Serving in the state assembly, 1776-79, he democratized Virginia's code of laws.

Virginia   Thomas Jefferson

His 1779 Bill for Establishing Religious Freedom was enacted into law in 1786. It established freedom of religion and the separation of church and state. It became the model for the First Amendment to the United States Constitution. It stated, in part:

"Almighty God hath created the mind free....

We the General Assembly of Virginia do enact that no man shall be compelled to frequent or support any religious worship, place, or ministry whatsoever... but that all men shall be free to profess...their opinions in matters of religion, and that the same shall in no wise...affect their civil liberties."

PROBLEMS OF THE CONFEDERATION

 The Confederation lasted only a few years: from 1781 to 1788.
What were the problems?
How would the Constitution solve them?

1. NO TAXING POWER—NO MONEY

The national government gradually went broke.
Why? The Confederation government could request money from the states, but it could not require them to pay taxes. So few did.

2. INFLATION

The Continental Congress had issued paper money to pay its $40,000,000 war debt.

These continental dollars were not backed by gold or silver, so their value was inflated: 40 paper dollars to 1 silver dollar.

Creditors avoided debtors trying to pay them with this worthless paper money, and hostility developed between the two groups.

3. TARIFF WARS

Each state, exercising its sovereignty, charged rival states a tariff (a tax on imported goods).

4. JEALOUSY AND QUARRELING AMONG STATES

Would warfare break out between the sovereign states, as it did frequently in Europe among sovereign nations?

5. FOREIGN AFFAIRS IN SHAMBLES

Each state had different trade regulations, a frustrating situation for foreign governments and businessmen.

Furthermore, foreign countries distrusted the Confederation because it had no power of the purse to back its agreements.

6. DISRESPECT FROM OTHER COUNTRIES

Monarchical nations, such as England and Spain, gleefully waited for the Confederation to fall apart. They were certain that the foolish idea of self-government would never work.

7. DEBTOR—CREDITOR CONFLICTS: SHAYS' REBELLION, 1787

In Massachusetts, debt-ridden farmers hurt by inflation couldn't meet payments on their farm mortgages. Rather than go to debtors' prison and/or lose their farms to creditors suing them in court to foreclose (claim the property as payment of the debt), a groups of farmers, led by Daniel Shays, took up arms against the courts.

George Washington, considering the Confederation's problems, feared the worst. In 1784 he had written:

> I PREDICT THE WORST CONSEQUENCES FROM A HALF-STARVED, LIMPING GOVERNMENT, ALWAYS MOVING ON CRUTCHES AND TOTTERING AT EVERY STEP.

OH GEORGE, DON'T BE SUCH A PESSIMIST...

In 1787, hearing of Shays' Rebellion, Washington wrote,

"There must be lodged somewhere a supreme power [a national government], without which the union cannot be of long duration."

What would the Americans do?

THREE FRIENDS: A MEETING OF NATIONALIST MINDS

George Washington believed that only a strong, national government could save the states from political and financial ruin.

George Washington's nationalist view was shared by other American leaders, including his young friends **James Madison**, a fellow Virginian, and **Alexander Hamilton** of New York, his chief military aide during the Revolutionary War.

Madison and Hamilton had become friends as members of the Continental Congress in 1782, when both attempted—in vain—to strengthen the Confederation government.

James Madison

George Washington

Alexander Hamilton

The three friends shared views in person and through correspondence during the 1780s.

Individually and together, Washington, Madison, and Hamilton guided events toward a peaceful overthrow of the Articles of Confederation and the creation of a new constitution that achieved "a more perfect union"—which we still enjoy today, two centuries later.

Here's an idea: Instead of a <u>confederation</u> government—a league of sovereign states, what about a <u>federal</u> government—a union that divides powers between a strong national government and the states? Baron de Montesquieu, the French philosopher, said that concentration of power results in tyranny and that the division and balance of power results in freedom.

A liberal and energetic constitution, well guarded, might restore us to respectability.

There may have been some excuse for setting up a weak Confederation, but there is no excuse for continuing it. We must think continentally, as <u>nationalists</u>.

WASHINGTON   MADISON   HAMILTON

A BOLD PROPOSAL

Two conferences, one successful and the other a failure, led to an unexpected proposal from Alexander Hamilton.

1785—MOUNT VERNON CONFERENCE

George Washington helped solve an immediate problem of the Confederation. He hosted a meeting of Virginia and Maryland delegates to settle disputes over fishing rights and navigation improvements on the Potomac River.

The meeting was a success.

1786—ANNAPOLIS CONFERENCE

James (Jemmy) Madison, encouraged by Washington's success, arranged for the Virginia legislature to call a meeting of all thirteen states in Annapolis, Maryland. The purpose: to discuss interstate commerce.

The meeting failed because delegates from only five states came. Among them was Madison's friend Alexander Hamilton from New York.

ANNAPOLIS CONFERENCE PROPOSAL: A 1787 CONVENTION

Alexander Hamilton snatched victory from defeat.

He wrote a bold proposal for the group, asking Congress to convene all the states in Philadelphia in May 1787 to correct "such defects as may be discovered to exist" in the Articles of Confederation—and to find ways "to render the Constitution of the Federal Government adequate to the exigencies [urgent needs] of the Union."

Would Congress agree?

constitution—the fundamental laws or principles by which a nation is governed, usually embodied in a written document
govern—to direct, or control, in a straight, smooth course for the good of the whole

1607   1787   2010

"The most wonderful work ever struck off at a given time by the brain and purpose of man."

—William E. Gladstone

The Constitution of the United States of America
<u>Preamble</u>

*We the People of the United States,
in Order to form a more perfect Union,
establish Justice,
ensure domestic Tranquillity,
provide for the common defense,
promote the general Welfare, and
secure the Blessings of Liberty to ourselves and our Posterity,
do ordain and establish this
Constitution for the United States of America.*

"Let virtue, honor, the love of liberty...be...the soul of this constitution,
and it will become the source of great and extensive happiness to this and future generations.
Vice, ignorance, and want of vigilance will be the only enemies able to destroy it."

—John Jay

"In New England every citizen...is taught...his religion,
the history of his country,
and the leading features of its Constitution....
It is extremely rare to find a man
imperfectly acquainted with all these things,
and a person wholly ignorant of them is a phenonomenon."

—Alexis de Tocqueville, 1830

A CONVENTION OVERVIEW

Congress, meeting in New York City, reluctantly agreed to the Annapolis proposal. It called for a Federal Convention in Philadelphia on May 14, 1787, but carefully stated that the meeting was "for the sole...purpose of revising the Articles of Confederation."

Now—would the states agree to send delegates? Those undecided did so when they learned that George Washington would be a delegate, for the whole country trusted the beloved Revolutionary War hero. The *Pennsylvania Herald* wrote:

"If the plan is not a good one, it is impossible that either General Washington or Dr. Franklin would have recommended it."

So it seemed to all the states except Rhode Island which, protective of its state's rights, refused to participate.

And so, 12 states sent 55 delegates to meet at Philadelphia's State House, now called Independence Hall, where eleven years earlier, in 1776, the Declaration of Independence had been adopted. Disregarding Congress's mandate to revise the old **Articles of Confederation—based on state sovereignty—** they emerged after four months with something new: a **Constituion based on national sovereignty**, the framework for a federal republic. Thirty-nine of the delegates, or framers, signed the Constitution of the United States "to form a more perfect Union...and secure the Blessings of Liberty to ourselves and our Posterity."

WHO WERE THESE FRAMERS—THESE EXTRAORDINARY MEN OF REASON AND CREATIVITY?

THE 39 FRAMERS
WHO SIGNED THE CONSTITUTION OF THE UNITED STATES

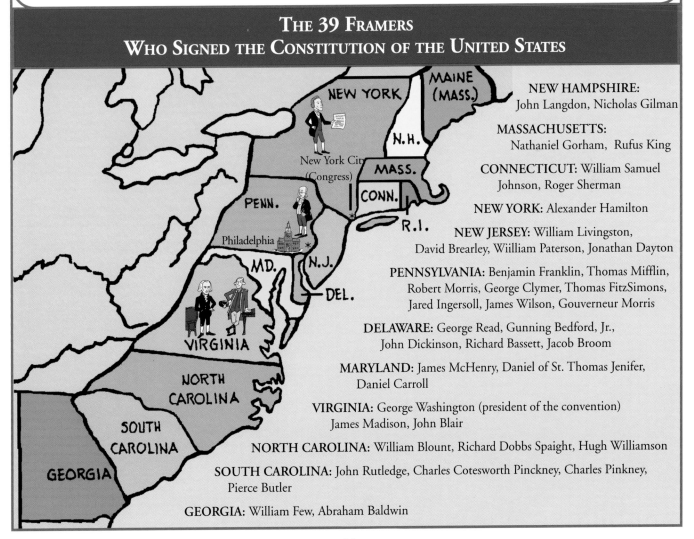

NEW HAMPSHIRE: John Langdon, Nicholas Gilman

MASSACHUSETTS: Nathaniel Gorham, Rufus King

CONNECTICUT: William Samuel Johnson, Roger Sherman

NEW YORK: Alexander Hamilton

NEW JERSEY: William Livingston, David Brearley, Wiilliam Paterson, Jonathan Dayton

PENNSYLVANIA: Benjamin Franklin, Thomas Mifflin, Robert Morris, George Clymer, Thomas FitzSimons, Jared Ingersoll, James Wilson, Gouverneur Morris

DELAWARE: George Read, Gunning Bedford, Jr., John Dickinson, Richard Bassett, Jacob Broom

MARYLAND: James McHenry, Daniel of St. Thomas Jenifer, Daniel Carroll

VIRGINIA: George Washington (president of the convention) James Madison, John Blair

NORTH CAROLINA: William Blount, Richard Dobbs Spaight, Hugh Williamson

SOUTH CAROLINA: John Rutledge, Charles Cotesworth Pinckney, Charles Pinkney, Pierce Butler

GEORGIA: William Few, Abraham Baldwin

James Madison: Father of the U.S. Constitution, 1751-1826

"Knowledge will forever govern ignorance; and a people who mean to be their own governors must arm themselves with the power which knowledge gives."—James Madison

Virginia delegate James "Jemmy" Madison arrived at the convention eleven days early, armed with a plan of action. Madison—a 36-year-old bachelor, shy, short (5'6"), soft-spoken, frail, and scholarly—was a man among men. Described by a contemporary as "no bigger than half a piece of soap," he nevertheless would emerge the clear leader of the 1787 Constitutional Convention, earning the title, **Father of the United States Constitution.**

Born in 1751 in Port Conway, Virginia, the eldest of 12 children, Madison grew up near Orange on his family's beautiful Virginia plantation Montpelier, which he later inherited. He studied at home with tutors, earned a degree in philosophy at Princeton in 1771, and then became a life-long statesman.

Madison served in the Virginia assembly (1776-77), where he and Thomas Jefferson began a 50-year friendship; the Confederation Congress (1780-83); and the U.S. Congress (1790-94). He served his country as secretary of state (1801-09) and president (1809-17). No wonder **Dolley Madison,** the vivacious Philadelphian he married in 1794, called him "the great little Madison."

Madison spent a year studying for the 1787 Convention, He was motivated by a central question:

"How can the country have a strong national government without taking freedom from the people?"

He read more than 200 books on history and philosophy (Aristotle, Voltaire, Locke, Montesquieu, Hume).

Many had been sent from France by his close friend **Thomas Jefferson,** who served as Minister to France from 1785 to 1789.

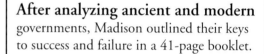

WOW! THE BOOKS I ORDERED ARE HERE!

YES SIR! A WHOLE WAGONLOAD!

After analyzing ancient and modern governments, Madison outlined their keys to success and failure in a 41-page booklet.

OVER 2,000 YEARS AGO, DEMOCRACY REIGNED IN THE GREEK CITY STATES AND THE ROMAN REPUBLIC. MADISON TRIED TO UNDERSTAND WHAT THESE GOVERNMENTS DID RIGHT...

...AND WHAT WENT WRONG!

Finally, Madison created a 15-point plan of government.
Arriving early in Philadelphia, he presented it to the other Virginia delegates, including **Governor Edmund Randolph** and **George Washington,** for their suggestions and endorsements.

HERE'S THE IDEA: INSTEAD OF A CONFEDERATION GOVERNMENT — A LEAGUE OF SOVEREIGN STATES, WHAT ABOUT A FEDERAL GOVERNMENT — A UNION THAT DIVIDES POWERS BETWEEN A STRONG NATIONAL GOVERNMENT AND THE STATES?

HMM...

MAKES SENSE.

MIGHT WORK.

Madison's 15-point "Virginia Plan" would provide the agenda for the entire proceedings of the Convention.

Modified by important compromises, it became the blueprint for the United States Constitution.

WHO'S THAT?

A MAN WITH A PLAN!

TO → STATE HOUSE

"...there never was an assembly of men...more...devoted to...devising...a constitutional system which would best... secure the permanent liberty and happiness of their country."—James Madison

In May 1787 the delegates slowly gathered for the FEDERAL CONVENTION in Philadelphia, Pennsylvania, at the STATE HOUSE—later called INDEPENDENCE HALL. Here in the same room eleven years earlier, in 1776, members of the Second Continental Congress had signed the Declaration of Independence.

Most of the 55 white, male delegates knew and respected one another through shared adventures.

3—had been in the Stamp Act Congress, 1765.

8—had signed the Declaration of Independence; 2, the Articles of Confederation.

42—had served in the First and/or Second Continental Congresses, 1774-1781.
    and/or the Confederation Congress, 1781-87.

30—were Revolutionary War veterans.

2—would be U.S. presidents (George Washington and James Madison); 1, a vice-president (Elbridge Gerry).

7—had been governors; 9 would be governors.

8—were judges; 2 would be chief justices of the Supreme Court.

2—were college presidents (Princeton and Columbia); 29 were college-educated.

34—had practiced law; 20 had helped write their state constitutions.

18—had worked or studied abroad; many were fluent in Latin, French, and other languages.

8—were born outside the U.S. but all within the British Empire.

Most were prosperous lawyers, businessmen, or plantation owners.

And they were young—average age, 42. Most were in their 30s—Madison, 36; Hamilton, 32.
Washington was 55. Benjamin Franklin, 81, was said to have the mind of a 25 year-old.

"This example of changing the constitution by assembling the wise men of the state, instead of assembling armies, will be worth as much to the world as the former examples we have given it."—Thomas Jefferson

Madison's Virginia Plan had to wait a few days because spring rains and muddy roads delayed many delegates.

The Convention officially began two weeks late on Friday, May 25, 1787, with a quorum of seven states.

During its hot, 4-month schedule of 6-hour meetings, six days a week, 13 of the 55 delegates withdrew for personal or policy reasons. The Convention rarely drew more than 30 to 35 delegates at a time.

The first day: George Washington, unanimously elected president of the Convention, took his presiding chair, saying...

On Monday, May 28, 1787, the delegates got down to business. Luckily for us, James Madison decided to sit up front and record for posterity every word said.

His journal, *Notes of Debates in the Federal Convention of 1787* (published in 1840, four years after his death), offers you a ringside seat at the Convention—next to him.

The delegates were old hands at running an effective meeting. Their rules of procedure included:

1. SECRECY

Delegates could not tell anyone about the proceedings until the Convention ended. This allowed them to speak freely and experiment with ideas.

Amazingly there were no leaks— perhaps because of an early scolding by George Washington, when he discovered a delegate's lost notes.

Washington threw the notes on a table, saying, "Let him who owns it take it," and stalked out. No one moved to recover the notes—to this day!

2. FLEXIBILITY

No votes were final until the last day, so delegates could change their minds freely. Every issue could be re-voted if anyone wished. More than 569 votes eventually were taken.

3. COURTESY

"Every member, rising to speak, shall address the President; and whilst he shall be speaking, none shall pass between them, or hold discourse or read a book, pamphlet, or paper...."

After the convention a member would remark in amazement:

Yet, quite often the convention debates grew fierce and tempers short.

Of course, who _would_ misbehave with the dignified, respected Washington seated on the platform, influencing the delegates with his slightest expression of pain or pleasure?

As **John Adams** once said of the regal Virginian:

"Next to Washington, a king would look like a valet."

Well, jovial Gouverneur Morris boasted one night that he was not intimidated by Washington. He bet Alexander Hamilton and other friends that he would dare greet Washington with a slap on the back.

The next day, more sober, he merely put his hand on Washington's shoulder, then regretted that!

VIRGINIA PLAN

On Tuesday, May 29, Virginia Governor Edmund Randolph presented the bold, 15-point Virginia Plan, outlining a national republican government with THREE BRANCHES:

1) EXECUTIVE
2) JUDICIARY
3) LEGISLATIVE,
   with population determining the number of members in both houses of the legislature.

The Virginia Plan caused shock waves!

Most delegates favored strengthening the central government by giving it powers to tax and control commerce. But they were divided between large-state "**nationalists**," who wanted even greater central powers, and small-state "**states' righters**," who wanted only to strengthen the Confederation, not overthrow it.

NEW JERSEY PLAN

William Paterson of New Jersey presented the small states' New Jersey Plan, which called for merely strengthening the Articles of Confederation, thus retaining state sovereignty.

Gunning Bedford of Delaware challenged the large-state delegates:

Alexander Hamilton's Plan

Then, out of the blue, Alexander Hamilton of New York presented a third plan that—to everyone's surprise–was modeled on the British government, which he admired.

The delegates listened politely to Hamilton for six hours,

then without comment began to debate the Virginia and New Jersey Plans.

COMPROMISE, COMPROMISE, COMPROMISE

NATIONAL VS. STATE SOVEREIGNTY

Virginia Plan vs. New Jersey Plan:

The delegates voted 7 to 3 for the **Virginia Plan.**

They realized this meant a revolutionary overthrow of the Confederation—and state sovereignty.

But the small states objected to the Virginia Plan's population-based legislature. They said the large states would have more people, thus more members and votes in Congress, thus more power than the small states.

Things were at a stalemate. Benjamin Franklin urged the two sides to **compromise,** each giving in a little.

LARGE STATE–SMALL STATE COMPROMISE

Roger Sherman of Connecticut offered a compromise:

This **Connecticut Compromise,** (including the House of Representatives' power to originate money bills), along with the North-South compromises described below, passed 5-4 as the Great Compromise.

Here's how Sherman's plan would work in the case of **Pennsylvania** (pop. 434,373) and **Delaware** (pop. 59,096):

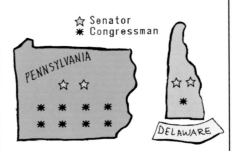

☆ Senator
✳ Congressman

By compromising—each side "shaving" some demands in order to reach agreement— the Convention was saved: a valuable lesson!

Solution to this conflict raised a new one—**between Northern and Southern states:** how to count the slave population in apportioning members of the House of Representatives.

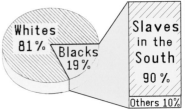

ESTIMATED U.S. POPULATION, 1790*

*These figures are from the 1790 U.S. census, which shows 757,181 African-Americans in a total population of 3,929,625.

NORTH-SOUTH COMPROMISES

Southern delegates wanted slaves to count as people so as to have more congressmen representing their states.

Northern delegates called this 1) unfair and 2) inconsistent because slaves were considered property.

Gouverneur Morris voiced a moral protest:

1. THREE-FIFTHS COMPROMISE

The delegates compromised in a strange way: a slave would count as 3/5 person in determining House representation and direct taxes (taxes owed by states to the federal government).

2. SLAVE TRADE COMPROMISE

Prohibition of slave imports would be delayed for 20 years, but until then (1807) slaveholders could be taxed up to $10.00 per imported slave.

Thus, the Constitution implicitly recognized slavery. However, in 1807 Congress abolished slave importation, and in 1865 the 13th Amendment to the Constitution abolished slavery. (The word "slave" is never used in the Constitution. Instead, phrases such as "other persons" and "such persons" refer to slaves.)

MORE COMPROMISES

AN IRONY: Several of the delegates were against slavery (including Washington, Madison, Hamilton, Franklin, and Mason). But they had to choose between having a constitution and ending slavery. Why? South Carolina and Georgia would not join the new nation without slavery.

As Abraham Lincoln said seven decades later, the word slavery was "hid away in the Constitution, just as an afflicted man hides away a ...cancer, which he dares not cut out at once, lest he bleed to death."

THE DELEGATES CHOSE TO HAVE AN IMPERFECT CONSTITUTION RATHER THAN NONE AT ALL. WHAT WOULD YOU HAVE DONE?

If avoiding the slavery question allowed for a constitution, it also threatened to destroy the constitution 70 years later with the Civil War.

THIS INFERNAL SLAVE TRAFFIC WILL BRING THE JUDGMENT OF HEAVEN ON A COUNTRY. PROVIDENCE PUNISHES NATIONAL SINS WITH NATIONAL CALAMITIES.

George Mason, author of the Virginia Bill of Rights, warned:

LEGISLATIVE COMPROMISE

Who should elect the legislators?

NOT THE PEOPLE! THEY CAN BE DUPED BY DEMAGOGUES! THE EVILS WE EXPERIENCE FLOW FROM THE EXCESS OF DEMOCRACY. HAMILTON, SHERMAN, AND G. MORRIS AGREE.

ELBRIDGE GERRY

I DISAGREE. A FREE GOVERNMENT MUST HAVE LEGISLATORS ELECTED BY THE PEOPLE AND ACCOUNTABLE TO THE PEOPLE. GEORGE MASON AND OTHERS THINK SO, TOO.

JAMES MADISON

THE COMPROMISE:

THE HOUSE OF REPRESENTATIVES WOULD BE ELECTED DIRECTLY BY THE PEOPLE.

THE SENATE WOULD BE ELECTED BY THE STATE LEGISLATORS.

(IN 1913 THE 17TH AMENDMENT PROVIDED FOR DIRECT ELECTION OF SENATORS BY THE PEOPLE.)

EXECUTIVE COMPROMISE

DECIDING TO HAVE A STRONG PRESIDENT WAS HARD FOR AMERICANS, WHO WERE FED UP WITH DESPOTIC KINGS. BUT EVERYONE KNEW WASHINGTON WOULD LIKELY BE THE FIRST PRESIDENT.

...AND GEORGE WOULD NEVER TRY TO BE A KING! BUT AFTER GEORGE, WHAT THEN?

Who should elect the president?

THE PEOPLE SHOULD VOTE FOR THE PRESIDENT.

NO. TOO MANY PEOPLE ARE UNEDUCATED. THIS WOULD BE AS UNNATURAL AS ASKING A BLIND MAN TO CHOOSE COLORS. PASSION AND DEMAGOGUERY WOULD PREVAIL OVER REASON!

JAMES WILSON

GEORGE MASON

It took 60 ballots to decide who should elect the president.

The compromise:

The president would be elected **indirectly** by the people through an **Electoral College** made up of electors chosen by each state— the number being equal to the number of its congressmen. The candidate with most votes would be president; the one with the next highest votes would be vice president.

(This was changed in 1804 by the 12th Amendment, which stated that the vice president would be elected on a separate ballot.)

THREE IMPORTANT QUESTIONS

SHOULD THERE BE RELIGIOUS REQUIREMENTS FOR PUBLIC OFFICE?—NO

"Among the most inestimable of our blessings is that...of liberty to worship our Creator in the way we think most agreeable in His will; a liberty deemed in other countries incompatible with good government and yet proved by our experience to be its best support.... The rights of conscience we never submitted [to government]. We are answerable for them to our God."—Thomas Jefferson

Eleven states did have religious requirements.

States:	To hold office one must:
Massachusetts and Maine—	be a Christian
NH, NJ, NC, SC, and GA—	be a Protestant Christian
Pennsylvania—	believe in God and the Bible
Delaware—	believe in the Christian Trinity

This meant that the 2,000 Jews and 25,000 Catholics in America—plus people of other faiths or of non-faith—did not qualify for public office in most states.

The delegates rejected the states' practice. Determined that government must not violate people's freedom to believe as they chose, they voted unanimously for Charles Pinckney's proposal.

NO RELIGIOUS TEST SHALL EVER BE REQUIRED AS A QUALIFICATION TO ANY OFFICE OR PUBLIC TRUST UNDER THE AUTHORITY OF THE UNITED STATES.

IT IS IMPOSSIBLE TO MAKE LAWS FOR THE HUMAN MIND. AS JEFFERSON SAID: ALMIGHTY GOD HATH CREATED THE MIND FREE.

Charles Pinckney

James Madison

WHO SHOULD DECLARE WAR? — CONGRESS

THE PRESIDENT, OF COURSE. HE WILL NOT MAKE WAR WITHOUT THE NATION'S SUPPORT.

WHAT! I NEVER EXPECTED TO HEAR IN A REPUBLIC A MOTION TO EMPOWER THE EXECUTIVE ALONE TO DECLARE WAR.

I AM AGAINST GIVING THE POWER OF WAR TO THE EXECUTIVE, BECAUSE HE IS NOT SAFELY TO BE TRUSTED WITH IT.... I AM FOR CLOGGING RATHER THAN FACILITATING WAR.

PIERCE BUTLER

GEORGE MASON

ELBRIDGE GERRY

THE COMPROMISE: CONGRESS HAS THE POWER TO DECLARE WAR; THE PRESIDENT HAS THE POWER TO REPEL SUDDEN ATTACKS.

U.S. CONSTITUTION

SHOULD THERE BE A STANDING ARMY—YES

"If we desire to secure peace,...it must be known that we are at all times ready for war." — George Washington

Americans were suspicious of standing armies in peacetime. They remembered Britain's "peacetime" army that had fired upon them at Lexington.

But Washington's aside comment in response to **Elbridge Gerry** gave another perspective.

AN ARMY IS DANGEROUS IN PEACETIME. I PROPOSE NO MORE THAN 3,000 TROOPS IN PEACETIME.

THEN I PROPOSE THAT NO ARMY INVADE THE U.S. WITH MORE THAN 3,000 TROOPS!

GEORGE WASHINGTON

THE COMPROMISE: THERE WOULD BE A STANDING ARMY BUT WITH A CIVILIAN —THE PRESIDENT— AS COMMANDER IN CHIEF AND WITH CONGRESS VOTING THE FUNDS.

U.S. CONSTITUTION

THE FINAL DAYS

July 24-August 7

Most of the delegates took a 10-day break while a 5-man **Committee of Detail** drafted a report of the Convention's resolves.

THINK I'LL GO FISHING.

COMMITTE OF DETAIL

The Committee of Detail consulted important documents on government, including the Magna Carta; colonial charters; the Albany Plan of Union; state constitutions; the Articles of Confederation; and a Native American document: THE GREAT LAW OF PEACE the Iroquois Confederacy's 200-year-old constitution.

Committee Chairman **John Rutledge** began the meeting by reading from the Iroquois Confederacy's constitution, which both he and Benjamin Franklin admired.

GENTLEMEN, THE IROQUOIS INDIANS' CONSTITUTION HAS ACHIEVED PEACE THROUGH UNION FOR OVER 200 YEARS BY ALLOWING TO EACH OF THE SIX IROQUOIS NATIONS SELF-GOVERNMENT IN INTERNAL AFFAIRS, WHILE UNITING THEM FOR EXTERNAL AFFAIRS. IT BEGINS: "WE, THE PEOPLE, TO FORM A UNION, TO ESTABLISH PEACE, EQUITY AND ORDER...."

GREAT LAW OF PEACE

August 7—The Committee of Detail submitted its report, organized into twenty-three articles. Then the delegates spent five weeks debating and revising it.

HOW LONG HAVE YOU BEEN HANGING AROUND HERE?

ALL SUMMER..... WAITING FOR THESE GUYS TO FINISH.

Pennsylvania State House

COMMITTEE OF STYLE—THE FINAL DRAFT

September 8-12—Gouverneur Morris led a 5-man Committee of Style (including Madison and Hamilton) in writing the final draft of the constitution.

Morris, a masterful writer steeped in the cadences of Shakespeare, distilled twenty-three rambling articles into seven—each clear, concise and eloquent.

Proud of his work, **Gouverneur Morris** commented:

HAVING REJECTED REDUNDANT AND EQUIVOCAL TERMS, I BELIEVED IT TO BE AS CLEAR AS OUR LANGUAGE WOULD PERMIT.

Later, Caleb Strong (delegate from Massachusetts) said, "For my part, I think the whole of it is expressed in the plain, common language of mankind."

September 12-17—The delegates fine-tuned the final draft, still voting on issues until the last day. **George Mason** had a last-minute idea, but the delegates unanimously rejected it. Tired and eager to go home, most agreed with **Roger Sherman**.

I THINK THE CONSTITUTION SHOULD HAVE A BILL OF RIGHTS. I CAN WRITE ONE IN NO TIME. REMEMBER, I WROTE THE ONE FOR VIRGINIA.

A BILL OF RIGHTS IS NOT NECESSARY, BECAUSE ALL POWERS NOT GRANTED TO THE GOVERNMENT ARE RESERVED FOR THE PEOPLE. BESIDES, 8 STATE CONSTITUTIONS ALREADY CONTAIN BILLS OF RIGHTS.

George Mason

Roger Sherman

THIS ALMOST FATAL ERROR LATER WOULD CAUSE NEAR-REJECTION OF THE CONSTITUTION IN THE RATIFYING PROCESS. ONLY A PROMISE TO ADD A BILL OF RIGHTS, BY AMENDMENT, RESCUED THE CONSTITUTION. IN 1791 THE PROMISE WOULD BE FULFILLED WITH THE FIRST TEN AMENDMENTS TO THE U.S. CONSTITUTION — THE BILL OF RIGHTS.

THE SIGNING

On September 17th, the delegates gathered for a final vote on the constitution. Would it pass? Benjamin Franklin rose with a speech in his hand. Too weak to stand, he asked James Wilson to read it for him.

Mr. President:

I confess that there are several parts of this Constitution which I do not at present approve, but I am not sure I shall never approve them. For having lived long, I have experienced many instances of being obliged by better information, or fuller consideration, to change opinions even on important subjects, which I once thought right, but found to be otherwise.

It is therefore that the older I grow, the more apt I am to doubt my own judgment, and to pay more respect to the judgment of others. Most men indeed, as well as most sects in religion, think themselves in possession of all truth, and that wherever others differ from them it is so far error....But though many persons think almost as highly of their own infallibility as of that of their sect, few express it so naturally as a certain French lady who in a dispute with her sister said, "I don't know how it happens, Sister, but I meet with nobody but myself that's always in the right."

In these sentiments, Sir, I agree to this Constitution with all its faults, if they are such....

I doubt too whether any other Convention we can obtain, may be able to make a better Constitution. For when you assemble a number of men to have the advantage of their joint wisdom, you inevitably assemble with those men all their prejudices, their passions, their errors of opinion, their local interest, and their selfish views. From such an assembly can a perfect production be expected?

It therefore astonishes me, Sir, to find this system approaching so near to perfection as it does; and I think it will astonish our enemies, who are waiting...to hear that our councils are confounded like those of the Builders of Babel....

Thus I consent, Sir, to this Constitution because I expect no better, and because I am not sure that it is not the best....On the whole, Sir, I cannot help expressing a wish that every member of the Convention who may still have objections to it would with me on this occasion doubt a little of his own infallibility, and, to make manifest our unanimity, put his name to this Instrument.

Washington then held the vote.

Each state had one vote. Every state voted "Aye," approving the Constitution by "the unanimous consent of the States present..."

Of the 42 delegates present, thirty-nine signed the document.

Three delegates chose not to sign: Mason, because it had no Bill of Rights; Randolph and Gerry, because they feared that not enough states would ratify it, and the result might be "confusion" if not "civil war."

(Later, Randolph supported the Constitution's ratification, and Gerry served under the Constitution as vice president.)

As the delegates came forward, one by one, to sign the Constitution, Benjamin Franklin looked at the sun on the president's chair and said:

I HAVE OFTEN GLANCED AT THIS SUN, WONDERING IF IT WERE RISING OR SETTING. NOW... I HAVE THE HAPPINESS TO KNOW THAT IT IS A RISING SUN.

"It appears to me, then, little short of a miracle, that the Delegates from so many different States, [different] in their manners, circumstances, and prejudices, should unite in forming a system of national government, so little liable to well founded objections."
—George Washington

Twin pillars—Capitalism and Democracy—uphold the ediface of the republic.

"Property must be secured, or liberty cannot exist."
—John Adams

UNITED STATES OF AMERICA

CAPITALISM
RIGHT TO:
PRIVATE PROPERTY
FREE ENTERPRISE
MAKE A PROFIT
ECONOMIC FREEDOM

DOOR OF OPPORTUNITY

DEMOCRACY
RIGHT TO:
LIBERTY
EQUALITY
JUSTICE
POLITICAL FREEDOM

If either pillar—Capitalism or Democracy—crumbles, the republic falls.

"Adieu to the security of property, adieu to the security of liberty."
—Alexander Hamilton

republic—a nation in which the supreme power rests in the people entitled to vote and is exercised by representatives elected directly or indirectly by them and responsible to them

federalism—a system of shared power between the states and the national government

A REPUBLIC WITH A FEDERAL SYSTEM AND POPULAR SOVEREIGNTY

As the delegates adjourned from the Constitutional Convention, a Philadelphia woman asked Benjamin Franklin:

The delegates had finished their work and emerged with the ultimate compromise: **a federal system** balancing dual citizenship in both state and national governments, each with its separate sphere and powers.

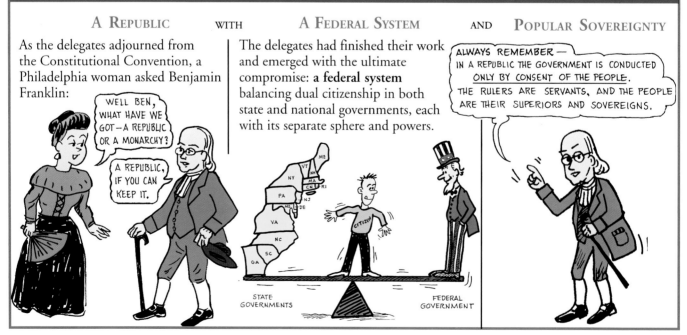

WELL BEN, WHAT HAVE WE GOT—A REPUBLIC OR A MONARCHY?

A REPUBLIC, IF YOU CAN KEEP IT.

ALWAYS REMEMBER—IN A REPUBLIC THE GOVERNMENT IS CONDUCTED ONLY BY CONSENT OF THE PEOPLE. THE RULERS ARE SERVANTS, AND THE PEOPLE ARE THEIR SUPERIORS AND SOVEREIGNS.

STATE GOVERNMENTS

FEDERAL GOVERNMENT

ratify—to approve by voting; constitution—the fundamental law providing a framework for government

ARTICLE VII OF THE CONSTITUTION SAYS:

"The ratification of the Conventions of nine states shall be sufficient for the establishment of this Constitution between the states so ratifying the same."

The miracle at Philadelphia would prove unreal unless framers of the Constitution could convince people to approve the Constitution. So take it to the people they did, by-passing the Confederation Congress and state legislatures in favor of state ratifying conventions with elected delegates.

On September 18, 1787, the Constitution was sent to the Confederation Congress in New York, which agreed to send copies to the thirteen states for ratification. On June 21, 1788, New Hampshire became the ninth state to ratify the Constitution, making it the supreme law of the land—by the supreme authority of the people themselves.

FEDERALISTS VS. ANTI-FEDERALISTS

The nine-month struggle for ratification pitted supporters of the Constitution, called **Federalists**, against opponents, called **Anti-Federalists**. Anti-Federalists included George Mason, a Convention delegate, and Patrick Henry,

THE FEDERALIST PAPERS

Three articulate Federalists—**Alexander Hamilton, James Madison**, and **John Jay**—turned the tide with a series of 85 convincing newspaper essays, published under the pseudonym **Publius**. The essays are the best commentaries ever written on the United States government.

RATIFYING THE CONSTITUTION

Ratification was a close call, as you can see! Success came only with the Federalists' promise to amend the Constitution with a **Bill of Rights**.

STATE	DATE RATIFIED	FOR–AGAINST
Delaware	Dec. 7, 1787	unanimous
Pennsylvania	Dec. 12, 1787	46—23
New Jersey	Dec. 18, 1787	unanimous
Georgia	Jan 2, 1788	unanimous
Connecticut	Jan. 9, 1788	128—40
Massachusetts	Feb. 6. 1788	187—168
Maryland	Apr. 26, 1788	63—11
South Carolina	May 23, 1788	149—73
New Hampshire	June 21, 1788	57—47
Virginia	June 25, 1788	89—79
New York	July 26, 1788	30—27
North Carolina	Nov. 21, 1789	195—77
Rhode Island	May 29, 1790	34—32

June 21, 1788 — New Hampshire, the ninth state to approve, cast the deciding vote for ratification.

WHAT DO WE HAVE?

Just what did the Americans ratify June 21, 1788, as the supreme law of the land?

The national government is located in Washington, District of Columbia, a site chosen by President George Washington in 1790.

THE CONSTITUTION OF THE UNITED STATES OF AMERICA

Preamble

We the People of the United States,
in Order to form a more perfect Union,
establish Justice, ensure domestic Tranquillity, provide for the
common defense, promote the general Welfare, and secure
the Blessings of Liberty to ourselves and our Posterity,
do ordain and establish this
Constitution for the United States of America.

BRANCHES OF GOVERNMENT

LEGISLATIVE	EXECUTIVE	JUDICIAL
Article I	Article II	Article III
CONGRESS	**PRESIDENT**	**SUPREME COURT**
MAKES LAWS (meets in the Capitol)	**EXECUTES LAWS** (lives and works at the White House)	**INTERPRETS LAWS,** THE CONSTITUTION, AND TREATIES OF THE U.S. IN DECIDING CERTAIN CASES. (meets in the Supreme Court Building)

Senate — **House of Representatives**

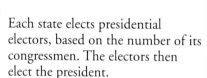

Two senators from each state, regardless of population, are elected for 6-year terms.	House members are elected from states in proportion to population for 2-year terms.	Each state elects presidential electors, based on the number of its congressmen. The electors then elect the president.	The president appoints judges, with advice and consent of the Senate. The term of office for the nine justices (originally there were only six) is for life—during good behavior.

Senate Committees	House Committees

Cabinet Departments
(created by Congress)

Lower Federal Courts
(created by Congress):
12 Circuit Courts of Appeal
94 District Courts

Agri-culture 1889	Commerce 1913	Defense 1949 (Dept. of War 1789)	Education 1979	Energy 1977	Health & Human Services 1953	Interior 1849	Housing & Urban Development 1965	Justice 1870	Labor 1913	State 1789	Transportation 1966	Treasury 1789	Veterans' Affairs 1989

THE THREE BRANCHES OF GOVERNMENT

"A legislative, an executive, and a judicial power
comprehend the whole of what is meant and understood by government.
It is by balancing each of these powers against the other two that the
efforts of human nature towards tyranny can alone be checked."
—John Adams

SEPARATION OF POWERS
AND
A SYSTEM OF CHECKS AND BALANCES

In addition to its own separate powers, each of the three branches of government is empowered to check the other two— in order to keep any branch from assuming too much power. This balance of national power allows for a strong central government, with safeguards to prevent its becoming tyrannical.

Article II

EXECUTIVE BRANCH POWERS

The President

1. Carries out the laws
2. Serves as commander in chief of the armed services
3. Appoints judges, ambassadors, and other officials
4. Makes treaties

(See Article II for additional powers.)

President can veto a bill proposed by Congress.

Congress can override veto with 2/3 vote of both houses.

President appoints Supreme Court judges.

Supreme Court can rule presidential actions unconstitutional.

Article I

LEGISLATIVE BRANCH POWERS

The Congress

Makes laws to:
1. Lay and collect taxes; pay the debts; provide for the common defense and general welfare of the United States
2. Regulate interstate and foreign commerce
3. Declare war

(See Article I for additional powers.)

Article III

JUDICIAL BRANCH

The Supreme Court

Judges cases of law and equity in accordance with:
1. the Constitution
2. the laws of the United States
3. treaties made by the United States.

Congress determines number of judges on Supreme Court.

Supreme Court can rule laws passed by Congress unconstitutional.

(See Article III for additional powers.)

THE FEDERAL SYSTEM: DIVISION OF POWERS

FEDERALISM— the division of powers between the national and state governments— reflects the Constitution's principle of limited government.

POWERS OF NATIONAL GOVERNMENT

♦ Regulate interstate and foreign commerce

♦ Coin money and regulate its value; fix standard of weights and measurments

♦ Punish counterfeiting of securities and current coin of the United States

♦ Set uniform rules of naturalization (process of becoming a U.S. citizen) and of bankruptcy (process of relieving debtors of debts they cannot pay)

♦ Establish post offices

♦ Promote science and useful arts with patents and copyrights

♦ Punish piracies and felonies on the high seas

♦ Declare war

♦ Raise and support an army

♦ Provide and maintain a navy

♦ Make rules for governing armed forces

♦ Call out state militias to execute U.S. laws, end rebellions, and repel invasions

♦ Share governance of militias with states

♦ Govern the national seat of government, a district separate from the states, not to exceed ten square miles (Washington D. C.)

♦ Govern territories and admit new states

♦ Make all laws which shall be necessary and proper for carrying into execution the foregoing powers

CONCURRENT POWERS OF NATIONAL AND STATE GOVERNMENTS

• Lay and collect taxes; pay debts

• Borrow money

• Provide for the general welfare

• Establish courts

• Enforce laws

• Punish lawbreakers

• Charter banks

• Make bankruptcy laws

• Build roads

POWERS RESERVED FOR THE STATES

♦ Establish local governments

♦ Conduct elections

♦ Regulate commerce within a state

♦ Establish and maintain schools

♦ Make marriage and divorce laws

♦ Provide for public safety

♦ Make laws regarding contracts, corporations, wills

♦ Raise and support a militia

OH YES — ONE THING MORE: THE 10TH AMENDMENT GAVE TO THE STATES "RESERVE POWER." THAT MEANS THE STATES OR THE PEOPLE HAVE ALL POWERS NOT GIVEN TO THE FEDERAL GOVERNMENT OR PROHIBITED TO THE STATES.

AMENDING THE CONSTITUTION

amend—to change
amendment—a change made in a motion, bill, or constitution
propose—to put forth for consideration
ratify—to approve by voting

Article V in the Constitution sets forth a two-step procedure for amending the Constitution.

Step One: PROPOSING the amendment
Step Two: RATIFYING the amendment

STEP ONE

AMENDMENTS SHALL BE PROPOSED IN EITHER OF TWO WAYS:

OR

BY CONGRESS
whenever two-thirds
of both Houses deem
it necessary

BY A CONVENTION
called by Congress on the
application of two-thirds
of the state legislatures

STEP TWO

AMENDMENTS SHALL BE RATIFIED IN EITHER OF TWO WAYS:

OR

BY LEGISLATURES
of three-fourths
of the states

BY CONVENTIONS
in three-fourths of the states
(whichever mode of ratification
may be proposed by Congress)

In more than two centuries, the Constitution of the United States has been amended only 27 times. All 27 amendments have been proposed by Congress.

The first 10 amendments—the BILL OF RIGHTS, protecting individual rights—were ratified in 1791.
The last amendment—the 27th—was ratified in 1992.

Purposes of the amendments include correcting the original articles (XI, XII, XX) and other changes, such as:
economic (XVI, federal income tax),
social (XVIII, XXI, the prohibition of alchohol and its repeal), and
political (XIII, abolishment of slavery; XIV, equality of citizenship rights; XVII, direct election of senators; XXII, 2-term limit for the presidency; XV, XIX, XXIV, reduced suffrage requirements regarding race, gender, age).

THE BILL OF RIGHTS: 1ST AMENDMENT

To make sure the new national government could not violate individual rights of the people—some dating back to the Magna Carta, Americans insisted that the U.S. Constitution be amended to include a bill (or listing) of these rights, guaranteeing them. Several states made this a condition for ratification. In 1789, Congressman James Madison led the House of Representatives in recommending such amendments to the states for ratification. **In 1791, the states ratified the first ten amendments to the Constitution—the Bill of Rights.**

THE BILL OF RIGHTS: 2ND–10TH AMENDMENTS

2ND AMENDMENT
Right to bear arms

3RD AMENDMENT
Right not to quarter soldiers

4TH AMENDMENT
Freedom from unreasonable search and seizure

5TH AMENDMENT
Due process of law

6TH AMENDMENT
Right to a speedy trial

7TH AMENDMENT
Right to trial by jury

8TH AMENDMENT
No cruel or unusual punishment

9TH AMENDMENT
Constitutional rights do not deny other rights.

10TH AMENDMENT
States' rights

How a Bill Becomes a Law

Article I, Section 7	A bill is a proposal for a new law.

To become a law, a bill must pass both houses of Congress (the House of Representatives and the Senate) and be signed by the president. The idea for a law can come from anyone—individuals, interest groups, the president of the United States—but only a member of the House of Representatives or Senate can sponsor a bill and guide it through the required steps.

ORIGIN—Most bills can originate (be introduced) in either house of Congress or in both houses at the same time. But **money bills** must originate in the House of Representatives.

COMMITTEES—About 10,000 bills per year are introduced. Each is given a number and assigned to a standing, or permanent, committee—such as agriculture, energy, or labor.

There are 22 committees in the House of Representatives and 15 in the Senate; each has several sub-committees. A bill might be 1,000 pages long and involve 200 people in 15 subcommittees.

HEARINGS—Subcommittees hold hearings at which experts and interested parties speak for or against the bill. The subcommittee then makes recommendations about the bill to the full committee.

COMMITTEE ACTION—The full committee can: 1) approve, 2) rewrite and approve, 3) amend (change) and approve, 4) reject the bill. (Only about 1,000 of 10,000 bills considered per year become laws; most die in committee.) If approved, the bill goes to the house of origin for debate.

CONGRESSIONAL ACTION—Back in its house of origin the bill is debated, perhaps amended, and voted on. If passed, it goes to the other house for the same action. If both houses approve the final bill, it goes to the president.

EXECUTIVE ACTION—

The president may: 1) sign the bill, making it a law

2) veto the bill

3) hold the bill without signing. Unsigned, it becomes a law in 10 days if Congress is in session. It dies if Congress adjourns before 10 days (a pocket veto).

If the president vetoes a bill, Congress can override the veto, and the bill becomes a law without the president's approval.

JUDICIAL ACTION—If a law does not conform to the United States Constitution, the Supreme Court has the power to declare the law unconstitutional.

PART THREE

The Declaration of Independence

"I have never had a feeling, politically, that did not spring from sentiments embodied in the Declaration of Independence."

—President Abraham Lincoln, 1861

The Constitution of the United States of America

"In New England every citizen...is taught...his religion, the history of his country, and the leading features of its Constitution....It is extremely rare to find a man imperfectly acquainted with all these things, and a person wholly ignorant of them is a phenonomenon."

—Alexis de Tocqueville, 1830

Anti-Federalist and Federalist Writings

"We are persuaded that the people of so large a continent, so different in interests, so distinct in habits, cannot...legislate in one body...."

—John Mercer

STATE GOVERNMENTS

FEDERAL GOVERNMENT

"Providence has been pleased to give this one connected country to one united people...."

—John Jay

In Congress, July 4, 1776
The Unanimous Declaration of the Thirteen United States of America

When in the Course of human events, it becomes necessary for one people to dissolve the political bands which have connected them with another, and to assume among the powers of the earth, the separate and equal station to which the Laws of Nature and of Nature's God entitle them, a decent respect to the opinions of mankind requires that they should declare the causes which impel them to the separation.

We hold these truths to be self-evident, that all men are created equal, that they are endowed by their Creator with certain unalienable Rights, that among these are Life, Liberty and the pursuit of Happiness. That to secure these rights, Governments are instituted among Men, deriving their just powers from the consent of the governed, That whenever any Form of Government becomes destructive of these ends, it is the Right of the People to alter or to abolish it, and to institute new Government, laying its foundation on such principles and organizing its powers in such form, as to them shall seem most likely to effect their Safety and Happiness. Prudence, indeed, will dictate that Governments long established should not be changed for light and transient causes; and accordingly all experience hath shown, that mankind are more disposed to suffer, while evils are sufferable, than to right themselves by abolishing the forms to which they are accustomed. But when a long train of abuses and usurpations, pursuing invariably the same Object evinces a design to reduce them under absolute Despotism, it is their right, it is their duty, to throw off such Government, and to provide new Guards for their future security. Such has been the patient sufferance of these Colonies; and such is now the necessity which constrains them to alter their former Systems of Government. **The history of the present King of Great Britain is a history of repeated injuries and usurpations, all having in direct object the establishment of an absolute Tyranny over these States. To prove this, let Facts be submitted to a candid world.**

He has refused his Assent to Laws, the most wholesome and necessary for the public good.

He has forbidden his Governors to pass Laws of immediate and pressing importance, unless suspended in their operation till his Assent should be obtained; and when so suspended, he has utterly neglected to attend to them.

He has refused to pass other Laws for the accommodation of large districts of people, unless those people would relinquish the right of Representation in the Legislature, a right inestimable to them and formidable to tyrants only.

He has called together legislative bodies at places unusual, uncomfortable, and distant from the depository of their Public Records, for the sole purpose of fatiguing them into compliance with his measures.

He has dissolved Representative Houses repeatedly, for opposing with manly firmness his invasions on the rights of the people.

He has refused for a long time, after such dissolutions, to cause others to be elected; whereby the Legislative powers, incapable of Annihilation, have returned to the People at large for their exercise; the State remaining in the mean time exposed to all the dangers of invasion from without, and convulsions within.

He has endeavoured to prevent the population of these States; for that purpose obstructing the Laws for Naturalization of Foreigners; refusing to pass others to encourage their migrations hither, and raising the conditions of new Appropriations of Lands.

He has obstructed the Administration of Justice, by refusing his Assent to Laws for establishing Judiciary powers.

He has made Judges dependent on his Will alone, for the tenure of their offices, and the amount and payment of their salaries.

He has erected a multitude of New Offices, and sent hither swarms of Officers to harass our people, and eat out their substance.

He has kept among us, in times of peace, Standing Armies without the Consent of our legislatures.

He has affected to render the Military independent of and superior to the Civil power.

He has combined with others to subject us to a jurisdiction foreign to our constitution, and unacknowledged by our laws; giving his Assent to their Acts of pretended Legislation:

For quartering large bodies of armed troops among us:

For protecting them, by a mock Trial, from Punishment for any Murders which they should commit on the Inhabitants of these States:

For cutting off our Trade with all parts of the World:

For imposing Taxes on us without our Consent:

For depriving us in many cases, of the benefits of Trial by Jury:

For transporting us beyond Seas to be tried for pretended offences:

For abolishing the free System of English Laws in a neighbouring Province, establishing therein an Arbitrary government, and enlarging its Boundaries so as to render it at once an example and fit instrument for introducing the same absolute rule into these Colonies:

For taking away our Charters, abolishing our most valuable Laws, and altering fundamentally the Forms of our Government:

For suspending our own Legislatures, and declaring themselves invested with Power to legislate for us in all cases whatsoever.

He has abdicated Government here, by declaring us out of his Protection and waging War against us.

He has plundered our seas, ravaged our Coasts, burnt our towns, and destroyed the lives of our people.

He is at this time transporting large Armies of foreign Mercenaries to compleat the works of death, desolation and tyranny, already begun with circumstances of Cruelty and perfidy scarcely paralleled in the most barbarous ages, and totally unworthy the Head of a civilized nation.

He has constrained our fellow Citizens taken Captive on the high Seas to bear Arms against their Country, to become the executioners of their friends and Brethren, or to fall themselves by their Hands.

He has excited domestic insurrections amongst us, and has endeavoured to bring on the inhabitants of our frontiers, the merciless Indian Savages, whose known rule of warfare, is an undistinguished destruction of all ages, sexes and conditions.

In every stage of these Oppressions We have Petitioned for Redress in the most humble terms: Our repeated Petitions have been answered only by repeated injury. A Prince, whose character is thus marked by every act which may define a Tyrant, is unfit to be the ruler of a free people.

Nor have We been wanting in our attentions to our British brethren. We have warned them from time to time of attempts by their legislature to extend an unwarrantable jurisdiction over us. We have reminded them of the circumstances of our emigration and settlement here. We have appealed to their native justice and magnanimity, and we have conjured them by the ties of our common kindred to disavow these usurpations, which, would inevitably interrupt our connections and correspondence. They too have been deaf to the voice of justice and of consanguinity. We must, therefore, acquiesce in the necessity, which denounces our Separation, and hold them, as we hold the rest of mankind, Enemies in War, in Peace Friends.

We, Therefore, the Representatives of the united States of America, in General Congress, Assembled, appealing to the Supreme Judge of the world for the rectitude of our intentions, do, in the Name, and by the Authority of the good People of these Colonies, solemnly publish and declare, That these United Colonies are, and of Right ought to be, Free and Independent States; that they are Absolved from all Allegiance to the British Crown, and that all political connection between them and the State of Great Britain, is and ought to be totally dissolved; and that as Free and Independent States, they have full Power to levy War, conclude Peace, contract Alliances, establish Commerce, and to do all other Acts and Things which Independent States may of right do. And for the support of this Declaration, with a firm reliance on the protection of divine Providence, we mutually pledge to each other our Lives, our Fortunes, and our sacred Honor.

PREAMBLE

We the People of the United States, in Order to form a more perfect Union, establish Justice, insure domestic Tranquility, provide for the common defence, promote the general Welfare, and secure the Blessings of Liberty to ourselves and our Posterity, do ordain and establish this Constitution for the United States of America.

ARTICLE I: THE LEGISLATIVE BRANCH

Section 1. All legislative Powers herein granted shall be vested in a Congress of the United States, which shall consist of a Senate and House of Representatives.

Section 2. The House of Representatives shall be composed of Members chosen every second Year by the People of the several States, and the Electors in each State shall have the Qualifications requisite for Electors of the most numerous Branch of the State Legislature.

No Person shall be a Representative who shall not have attained to the Age of twenty-five years, and have been seven Years a Citizen of the United States, and who shall not, when elected, be an Inhabitant of that State in which he shall be chosen.

Representatives and direct Taxes shall be apportioned among the several States which may be included within this Union, according to their respective Numbers, which shall be determined by adding to the whole Number of free Persons, including those bound to Service for a Term of Years, and excluding Indians not taxed, three-fifths of all other Persons. The actual Enumeration shall be made within three Years after the first Meeting of the Congress of the United States, and within every subsequent Term of ten Years, in such Manner as they shall by Law direct. The Number of Representatives shall not exceed one for every thirty Thousand, but each State shall have at Least one Representative; and until such enumeration shall be made, the State of New Hampshire shall be entitled to choose three, Massachusetts eight, Rhode Island and Providence Plantations one, Connecticut five, New York six, New Jersey four, Pennsylvania eight, Delaware one, Maryland six, Virginia ten, North Carolina five, South Carolina five, and Georgia three.

When vacancies happen in the Representation from any State, the Executive Authority thereof shall issue Writs of Election to fill such Vacancies.

The House of Representatives shall choose their Speaker and other Officers; and shall have the sole Power of Impeachment.

Section 3. The Senate of the United States shall be composed of two Senators from each State, chosen by the Legislature thereof, for six Years; and each Senator shall have one Vote.

Immediately after they shall be assembled in Consequence of the first Election, they shall be divided as equally as may be into three Classes. The Seats of the Senators of the first Class shall be vacated at the Expiration of the second Year, of the second Class at the Expiration of the fourth Year, and of the third Class at the Expiration of the sixth Year, so that one third may be chosen every second Year; and if Vacancies happen by Resignation, or otherwise, during the Recess of the Legislature of any State, the Executive thereof may make temporary Appointments until the next Meeting of the Legislature, which shall then fill such Vacancies.

No Person shall be a Senator who shall not have attained to the Age of thirty Years, and been nine Years a Citizen of the United States, and who shall not, when elected, be an Inhabitant of that State for which he shall be chosen.

The Vice President of the United States shall be President of the Senate, but shall have no Vote, unless they be equally divided.

The Senate shall choose their other Officers, and also a President pro tempore, in the absence of the Vice President, or when he shall exercise the Office of President of the United States.

The Senate shall have the sole Power to try all Impeachments. When sitting for that Purpose, they shall be on Oath or Affirmation. When the President of the United States is tried, the Chief Justice shall preside: And no Person shall be convicted without the Concurrence of two thirds of the Members present.

Judgment in Cases of Impeachment shall not extend further than to removal from Office, and disqualification to hold and enjoy any Office of Honor, Trust or Profit under the United States: but the Party convicted shall nevertheless be liable and subject to Indictment, Trial, Judgment and Punishment, according to Law.

Section 4. The Times, Places and Manner of holding Elections for Senators and Representatives, shall be prescribed in each State by the Legislature thereof; but the Congress may at any time by Law make or alter such Regulations, except as to the Place of choosing Senators.

The Congress shall assemble at least once in every Year, and such Meeting shall be on the first Monday in December, unless they shall by Law appoint a different Day.

Section 5. Each House shall be the Judge of the Elections, Returns and Qualifications of its own Members, and a Majority of each shall constitute a Quorum to do Business; but a smaller number may adjourn from day to day, and may be authorized to compel the Attendance of absent Members, in such Manner, and under such Penalties as each House may provide.

Each House may determine the Rules of its Proceedings, punish its Members for disorderly Behavior, and with the concurrence of two thirds, expel a Member.

Each House shall keep a Journal of its Proceedings, and from time to time publish the same, excepting such Parts as may in their Judgment require Secrecy; and the Yeas and Nays of the Members of either House on any question shall, at the Desire of one fifth of those Present, be entered on the Journal.

Neither House, during the Session of Congress, shall, without the Consent of the other, adjourn for more than three days, nor to any other Place than that in which the two Houses shall be sitting.

Section 6. The Senators and Representatives shall receive a Compensation for their Services, to be ascertained by Law, and paid out of the Treasury of the United States. They shall in all Cases, except Treason, Felony and Breach of the Peace, be privileged from Arrest during their Attendance at the Session of their respective Houses, and in going to and returning from the same; and for any Speech or Debate in either House, they shall not be questioned in any other Place.

No Senator or Representative shall, during the Time for which he was elected, be appointed to any civil Office under the authority of the United States, which shall have been created, or the Emoluments whereof shall have encreased during such time; and no Person holding any Office under the United States, shall be a Member of either House during his Continuance in Office.

Section 7. All Bills for raising Revenue shall originate in the House of Representatives; but the Senate may propose or concur with Amendments as on other Bills.

Every Bill which shall have passed the House of Representatives and the Senate, shall, before it become a Law, be presented to the President of the United States; If he approves he shall sign it, but if not he shall return it, with his Objections to that House in which it shall have originated, who shall enter the Objections at large on their Journal, and proceed to reconsider it. If after such Reconsideration two thirds of that House shall agree to pass the bill, it shall be sent, together with the Objections, to the other House, by which it shall likewise be reconsidered, and if approved by two thirds of that House, it shall become a Law. But in all such Cases the votes of both Houses shall be determined by Yeas and Nays, and the Names of the Persons voting for and against the Bill shall be entered on the Journal of each House respectively. If any Bill shall not be returned by the President within ten Days (Sundays excepted) after it shall have been presented to him, the Same shall be a Law, in like Manner as if he had signed it, unless the Congress by their Adjournment prevent its Return, in which Case it shall not be a Law.

Every Order, Resolution, or Vote to which the Concurrence of the Senate and House of Representatives may be necessary (except on a question of Adjournment) shall be presented to the President of the United States; and before the Same shall take Effect, shall be approved by him, or being disapproved by him, shall be repassed by two thirds of the Senate and House of Representatives, according to the Rules and Limitations prescribed in the Case of a Bill.

Section 8. The Congress shall have Power to lay and collect Taxes, Duties, Imposts and Excises, to pay the Debts and provide for the common Defence and general welfare of the United State; but all Duties, Imposts and Excises shall be uniform throughout the United States

To borrow money on the credit of the United States;

To regulate Commerce with foreign Nations, and among the several States, and with the Indian Tribes;

To establish a uniform rule of Naturalization, and uniform Laws on the subject of Bankruptcies throughout the United States;

To coin Money, regulate the Value thereof, and of foreign Coin, and fix the Standard of Weights and Measures;

To provide for the Punishment of counterfeiting the Securities and current Coin of the United States;

To establish Post Offices and post Roads;

To promote the Progress of Science and useful Arts, by securing for limited Times to Authors and Inventors the exclusive Right to their respective Writing and Discoveries;

To constitute Tribunals inferior to the Superior Court;

To define and punish Piracies and Felonies committed on the high Seas, and Offenses against the Law of Nations;

To declare War, grant Letters of Marque and Reprisal, and make Rules concerning Captures on Land and Water;

To raise and support Armies, but no Appropriation of Money to that Use shall be for a longer Term than two years;

To provide and maintain a Navy;

To make Rules for the Government and Regulation of the land and naval Forces;

To provide for calling forth the Militia to execute the Laws of the Union, suppress Insurrections and repel Invasions;

To provide for organizing, arming, and disciplining the Militia, and for governing such Part of them as may be employed in the Service of the United States, reserving to the States respectively, the Appointment of the Officers, and the Authority of training the Militia according to the discipline prescribed by Congress;

To Exercise the exclusive Legislation in all Cases whatsoever, over such District (not exceeding ten Miles square) as may, by Cession of particular States, and the acceptance of Congress, become the Seat of the Government of the United States, and to exercise like Authority over all Places purchased by the Consent of the Legislature of the State in which the Same shall be, for the Erection of Forts, Magazines, Arsenals, dock-Yards, and other needful Buildings; And

To make all Laws which shall be necessary and proper for carrying into Execution the foregoing Powers, and all other Powers vested by this Constitution in the Government of the United States, or in any Department or Officer thereof.

Section 9. The Migration or Importation of such Persons as any of the States now existing shall think proper to admit, shall not be prohibited by the Congress prior to the year one thousand eight hundred and eight, but a tax or duty may be imposed on such Importation, not exceeding ten dollars for each Person.

The privilege of the Writ of Habeas Corpus shall not be suspended unless when in Cases of Rebellion or Invasion the public Safety may require it.

No Bill of Attainder or ex post facto Law shall be passed.

No capitation, or other direct, Tax shall be laid, unless in Proportion to the Census of Enumeration herein before directed to be taken.

No capitation, or other direct, Tax shall be laid, unless in Proportion to the Census of Enumeration herein before directed to be taken.

No Tax or Duty shall be laid on Articles exported from any State.

No Preference shall be given by any Regulation of Commerce or Revenue to the Ports of one State over those of another; nor shall Vessels bound to, or from, one State, be obliged to enter, clear, or pay Duties in another.

No Money shall be drawn from the Treasury, but in Consequence of Appropriations made by Law; and a regular Statement and Account of the Receipts and Expenditures of all public Money shall be published from time to time.

No Title of Nobility shall be granted by the United States: And no Person holding any Office of Profit or Trust under them, shall, without the Consent of the Congress, accept of any present, Emolument, Office, or Title, of any kind whatever, from any King, Prince, or foreign State.

Section 10. No State shall enter into any Treaty, Alliance, or Confederation; grant Letters of Marque and Reprisal; coin Money; emit Bills of Credit; make any Thing but gold and silver Coin a Tender in Payment of Debts; pass any Bill of Attainder, ex post facto Law, or Law impairing the Obligation of Contracts or grant any Title of Nobility.

No State shall, without the Consent of the Congress, lay any Imposts or Duties on Imports or Exports, except what may be absolutely necessary for executing its inspection Laws: and the net Produce of all Duties and Imposts, laid by any State on Imports or Exports, shall be for the Use of the Treasury of the United States; and all such Laws shall be subject to the Revision and Control of the Congress.

No State shall, without the Consent of Congress, lay any duty of Tonnage, keep Troops, or Ships of War in time of Peace, enter into any Agreement or Compact with another State, or with a foreign Power, or engage in War, unless actually invaded, or in such imminent Danger as will not admit of delay.

ARTICLE II: EXECUTIVE DEPARTMENT

Section 1. The executive Power shall be vested in a President of the United States of America. He shall hold his Office during the Term of four Years, and, together with the Vice President, chosen for the same Term, be elected, as follows.

Each State shall appoint, in such Manner as the Legislature thereof may direct, a Number of Electors, equal to the whole Number of Senators and Representatives to which the State may be entitled in the Congress: but no Senator or Representative, or Person holding an office of Trust or Profit under the United States, shall be appointed an Elector.

The Electors shall meet in their respective States, and vote by Ballot for two persons, of whom one at least shall not be an Inhabitant of the same State with themselves. And they shall make a List of all the Persons voted for, and of the Number of Votes for each; which List they shall sign and certify, and transmit sealed to the Seat of the Government of the United States, directed to the President of the Senate. The President of the Senate shall, in the Presence of the Senate and House of Representatives, open all the Certificates, and the Votes shall then be counted. The person having the greatest Number of Votes shall be the President, if such Number be a Majority of the whole Number of Electors appointed; and if there be more than one who have such Majority, and have an equal number of Votes, then the House of Representatives shall immediately choose by Ballot one of them for President; and if no Person have a Majority, then from the five highest on the List the said House shall in like Manner choose the President. But in choosing the President, the Votes shall be taken by States, the Representation from each State having one Vote; a quorum for this Purpose shall consist of a Member or Members from two thirds of the States, and a Majority of all the States shall be necessary to a Choice. In every Case, after the Choice of the President, the Person having the Greatest Number of Votes of the Electors shall be the Vice President. But if there should remain two or more who have equal Votes, the Senate shall choose from them by Ballot the Vice President.

The Congress may determine the Time of choosing the Electors, and the Day on which they shall give their Votes; which Day shall be the same throughout the United States.

No person except a natural born Citizen, or a Citizen of the United States, at the time of the adoption of this Constitution, shall be eligible to the Office of President; neither shall any Person be eligible to that Office who shall not have attained to the Age of Thirty-five Years, and been fourteen Years a Resident within the United States. In a Case of the Removal of the President from Office, or of his Death, Resignation, or Inability to discharge the Powers and Duties of the said Office, the same shall devolve on the Vice-President, and the Congress may by Law provide for the Case of Removal, Death, Resignation or Inability, both of the President and the Vice President, declaring what Officer shall then act as President, and such Officer shall act accordingly, until the Disability be removed, or a President shall be elected.

The President shall, at stated Times, receive for his Services, a Compensation, which shall neither be encreased nor diminished during the Period for which he shall have been elected, and he shall not receive within that Period any other Emolument from the United States, or any of them.

Before he enter on the Execution of his Office, he shall take the following Oath or Affirmation: "I do solemnly swear (or affirm) that I will faithfully execute the Office of the President of the United States, and will to the best of my Ability, preserve, protect and defend the Constitution of the United States."

Section 2. The President shall be Commander in Chief of the Army and Navy of the United States, and of the Militia of the several States, when called into the actual Service of the United States; he may require the Opinion in writing, of the principal Officer in each of the executive Departments, upon any subject relating to the Duties of their respective Offices, and he shall have Power to Grant Reprieves and Pardons for Offenses against the United States, except in Cases of Impeachment.

He shall have Power, by and with the Advice and Consent of the Senate, to make Treaties, provided two thirds of the Senators present concur; and he shall nominate, and by and with the Advice and Consent of the Senate, shall appoint Ambassadors, other public Ministers and Consuls, Judges of the supreme Court, and all other Officers of the United States, whose Appointments are not herein otherwise provided for, and which shall be established by Law: but the Congress may by Law vest the Appointment of such inferior Officers, as they think proper, in the President alone, in the Courts of Law, or in the Heads of Departments.

The President shall have Power to fill up all Vacancies that may happen during the Recess of the Senate, by granting commissions which shall expire at the End of their next Session.

Section 3. He shall from time to time give to the Congress Information of the State of the Union, and recommend to their Consideration such Measures as he shall judge necessary and expedient; he may, on extraordinary Occasions, convene both Houses, or either of them, and in Case of Disagreement between them, with Respect to the Time of Adjournment, he may adjourn them to such Time as he shall think proper; he shall receive Ambassadors and other public Ministers; he shall take Care that the Laws be faithfully executed, and shall Commission all the Officers of the United States.

Section 4. The President, Vice President and all other civil Officers of the United States, shall be removed from Office on Impeachment for, and Conviction of, Treason, Bribery, or other high Crimes and Misdemeanors.

ARTICLE III: JUDICIAL DEPARTMENT

Section 1. The judicial Power of the United States, shall be vested in one supreme Court, and in such inferior Courts as the Congress may from time to time ordain and establish. The Judges, both of the supreme and inferior Courts, shall hold their offices during good Behavior, and shall, at stated Times, receive for their services, a Compensation, which shall not be diminished during their Continuance in Office.

Section 2. The judicial Power shall extend to all Cases, in Law and Equity, arising under this Constitution, the Laws of the United States, and Treaties made, or which shall be made, under their Authority;—to all

Cases affecting Ambassadors, other public Ministers and Consuls; all cases of admiralty and maritime Jurisdiction;—to Controversies to which the United States shall be a Party;—to Controversies between two or more States;—between a State and Citizens of another state;—between Citizens of different states;—between Citizens of the same State claiming Lands under Grants of different States, and between a State, or the Citizens thereof, and foreign States, Citizens or Subjects.In all Cases affecting Ambassadors, other public Ministers and Consuls, and those in which a State shall be Party, the supreme Court shall have original Jurisdiction. In all the other Cases before mentioned, the supreme Court shall have appellate Jurisdiction, both as to Law and Fact, with such Exceptions, and under such Regulations as the Congress shall make.

The trial of all Crimes, except in cases of Impeachment, shall be by Jury; and such Trial shall be held in the State where the said Crimes shall have been committed; but when not committed within any State, the Trial shall be at such Place or Places as the Congress may by Law have directed.

Section 3. Treason against the United States, shall consist only in levying War against them, or in adhering to their Enemies, giving them Aid and Comfort. No Person shall be convicted of Treason unless on the Testimony of two Witnesses to the same overt Act, or on Confession in open Court.

The Congress shall have Power to declare the Punishment of Treason, but no Attainder of Treason shall work Corruption of Blood, or Forfeiture except during the Life of the Person attainted.

ARTICLE IV: RELATIONS AMONG THE STATES

Section 1. Full Faith and Credit shall be given in each State to the public Acts, Records, and judicial Proceedings of every other State. And the Congress may by general Laws prescribe the Manner in which such Acts, Records and Proceedings shall be proved, and the Effect thereof.

Section 2. The Citizens of each State shall be entitled to all Privileges and Immunities of Citizens in the several States.

A Person charged in any State with Treason, Felony or other Crime, who shall flee from Justice, and be found in another State, shall on demand of the executive Authority of the State from which he fled, be delivered up, to be removed to the State having Jurisdiction of the Crime.

No Person held in Service or Labour in one State, under the laws thereof, escaping into another, shall, in Consequence of any Law or Regulation therein, be discharged from such Service or Labour, but shall be delivered up on Claim of the Party to whom such Service or Labour may be due.

Section 3. New States may be admitted by the Congress into this Union; but no new State shall be formed or erected within the Jurisdiction of any other State; nor any State be formed by the Junction of two or more States, or parts of States, without the Consent of Legislatures of the States concerned as well as of the Congress.

The Congress shall have Power to dispose of and make all needful Rules and Regulations respecting the Territory or other Property belonging to the United States; and nothing in this Constitution shall be so construed as to Prejudice any Claims of the United States, or of any particular State.

Section 4. The United States shall guarantee to every State in this Union a Republican Form of Government, and shall protect each of them against Invasion; and on Application of the Legislature, or of the Executive (when the Legislature cannot be convened) against domestic Violence.

ARTICLE V: AMENDING THE CONSTITUTION

The Congress, whenever two thirds of both Houses shall deem it necessary, shall propose Amendments to this Constitution, or, on the Application of the Legislatures of two thirds of the several States, shall call a Convention for proposing Amendments, which, in either Case, shall be valid to all Intents and Purposes, as part of this Constitution, when ratified by the Legislatures of three fourths of the several States, or by Conventions in three fourths thereof, as the one or the other Mode of Ratification may be proposed by the Congress: Provided that no Amendment which may be made prior to the Year One thousand eight hundred and eight shall in any Manner affect the first and fourth Clauses in the Ninth Section of the first Article; and that no State, without its consent, shall be deprived of its equal Suffrage in the Senate.

ARTICLE VI: GENERAL PROVISIONS

All Debts contracted and Engagements entered into, before the Adoption of this Constitution, shall be as valid against the United States under this Constitution, as under the Confederation.

This Constitution, and the Laws of the United States which shall be made in Pursuance thereof; and all Treaties made, or which shall be made, under the Authority of the United States, shall be the supreme law of the Land; and the Judges in every State shall be bound thereby, any Thing in the Constitution or Laws of any State to the Contrary notwithstanding.

The Senators and Representatives before mentioned, and the Members of the several State Legislatures, and all executive and judicial Officers, both of the United States and of the several States, shall be bound by Oath or Affirmation, to support this Constitution; but no religious Test shall ever be required as a Qualification to any Office or public Trust under the United States.

ARTICLE VII: RATIFICATION

The Ratification of the Conventions of nine States shall be sufficient for the Establishment of this Constitution between the States so ratifying the Same.

DONE in Convention by Unanimous Consent of the States present the Seventeenth Day of September in the Year of our Lord one thousand seven hundred and eighty-seven and of the Independence of the United States of America the Twelfth. In Witness whereof We have hereunto subscribed our Names.

AMENDMENTS
The first ten amendments to the Constitution, ratified by the states in 1791, are called the Bill of Rights.

AMENDMENT I (1791)

Congress shall make no law respecting an establishment of religion, or prohibiting the free exercise thereof: or abridging the freedom of speech, or of the press; or the right of the people peaceably to assemble, and to petition the Government for a redress of grievances.

AMENDMENT II (1791)

A well regulated Militia, being necessary to the security of a free State, the right of the people to keep and bear Arms, shall not be infringed.

AMENDMENT III (1791)

No soldier shall, in time of peace, be quartered in any house, without the consent of the Owner, nor in time of war, but in a manner to be prescribed by law.

AMENDMENT IV (1791)

The right of the people to be secure in their persons, houses, papers, and effects, against unreasonable searches and seizures, shall not be violated, and no Warrants shall issue, but upon probable cause, supported by Oath or affirmation, and particularly describing the place to be searched, and the persons or things to be seized.

AMENDMENT V (1791)

No person shall be held to answer for a capital, or otherwise infamous crime, unless on a presentment or indictment of a Grand Jury, except in cases arising in the land or naval forces, or in the Militia, when in actual service in time of War or public danger; nor shall any person be subject for the same offence to be twice put in jeopardy of life or limb; nor shall be compelled in any criminal case to be a witness against himself, nor be deprived of life, liberty, or property, without due process of law; nor shall private property be taken for public use, without just compensation.

AMENDMENT VI (1791)

In all criminal prosecutions, the accused shall enjoy the right to a speedy and public trial, by an impartial jury of the State and district wherein the crime shall have been committed, which district shall have been previously ascertained by law, and to be informed of the nature and cause of the accusation; to be confronted with the witnesses against him; to have compulsory process for obtaining witnesses in his favor, and to have the Assistance of Counsel for his defense.

AMENDMENT VII (1791)

In suits at common law, where the value in controversy shall exceed twenty dollars, the right of trial by jury shall be preserved, and no fact tried by a jury, shall be otherwise reexamined in any court of the United States, than according to rules of the common law.

AMENDMENT VIII (1791)

Excessive bail shall not be required, nor excessive fines imposed, nor cruel and unusual punishments inflicted.

AMENDMENT IX (1791)

The enumeration in the Constitution, of certain rights, shall not be construed to deny or disparage others retained by the people.

AMENDMENT X (1791)

The powers not delegated to the United States by the Constitution, nor prohibited by it to the States, are reserved to the States respectively, or to the people.

AMENDMENT XI 1798)

The Judicial power of the United States shall not be construed to extend to any suit in law or equity, commenced or prosecuted against one of the United States by Citizens of another State, or by Citizens or Subjects of any Foreign State.

AMENDMENT XII (1804)

The Electors shall meet in their respective states and vote by ballot for President and Vice-President, one of whom, at least, shall not be an inhabitant of the same state with themselves; they shall name in their ballots the person voted for as President, and in distinct ballots the person voted for as Vice-President, and they shall make distinct lists of all persons voted for as President, and of all persons voted for as Vice-President, and of the number of votes for each, which lists they shall sign and certify, and transmit sealed to the seat of the government of the United States, directed to the President of the Senate; The President of the Senate shall, in the presence of the Senate and House of Representative, open all the certificates and the votes shall then be counted; The person having the greatest number of votes for President, shall be the President, if such number be a majority of the whole number of Electors appointed; and if no person have such majority, then from the persons having the highest numbers not exceeding three on the list of those voted for a President, the House of Representatives shall choose immediately, by ballot, the President. But in choosing the President, the votes shall be taken by states, the representation from each state having one vote; a quorum for this purpose shall consist of a member or members form two-thirds of the states, and a majority of all the states shall be necessary to a choice. And if the House of Representatives shall not choose a President whenever the right of choice shall devolve upon them, before the fourth day of March next following, then the Vice-President shall act as President, as in the case of the death or other constitutional disability of the President: The person having the greatest number of votes as Vice-President, shall be the Vice-President, if such number be a majority of the whole number of Electors appointed, and if no person have a majority, then from the two highest number on the list, the Senate shall choose the Vice-President; a quorum for the purpose shall consist of two-thirds of the whole number of Senators, and a majority of the whole number shall be necessary to a choice. But no person constitutionally ineligible to the office of President shall be eligible to that of Vice-President of the United States.

AMENDMENT XIII (1865)

Section 1. Neither slavery nor involuntary servitude, except as a punishment for crime whereof the party shall have been duly convicted, shall exist within the United States, or any place subject to their jurisdiction.

Section 2. Congress shall have power to enforce this article by appropriate legislation.

AMENDMENT XIV (1868)

Section 1. All persons born or naturalized in the United States, and subject to the jurisdiction thereof, are citizens of the United States and of the State wherein they reside. No state shall make or enforce any law which shall abridge the privileges or immunities of citizens of the United States; nor shall any State deprive any person of life, liberty, or property, without due process of law; nor deny any person within its jurisdiction the equal protection of the laws.

Section 2. Representatives shall be apportioned among the several States according to their respective numbers, counting the whole number of persons in each State, excluding Indians not taxed. But when the right to vote at any election for the choice of electors for President and Vice-President of the United States, Representatives in Congress, the Executive and Judicial officers of a State, or the members of the Legislature thereof, is denied to any of the male inhabitants of such State, being twenty-one years of age, and citizens of the United States, or in any way abridged, except for participation in rebellion, or other crime, the basis of representation therein shall be reduced in the proportion which the number of such male citizens shall bear to the whole number of male citizens twenty-one years of age in such state.

Section 3. No person shall be a Senator or Representative in Congress, or elector of President and Vice-President, or hold any office, civil or military, under the United States, or under any State, who having previously taken an oath, as a member of Congress, or as an officer of the United States, or as a member of any State legislature, or as an executive or judicial officer of any State, to support the Constitution of the United States, shall have engaged in insurrection or rebellion against the same, or given aid or comfort to the enemies thereof. But Congress may by a vote of two-thirds of each House, remove such a disability.

Section 4. The validity of the public debt of the United States, authorized by law, including debts incurred for payment of pensions and bounties for services in suppressing insurrection or rebellion, shall not be questioned. But neither the United States nor any State shall assume or pay any debt or obligation incurred in aid of insurrection or rebellion against the United States, or any claim for the loss or emancipation of any slave; but all such debts, obligations and claims shall be held illegal and void.

Section 5. The Congress shall have power to enforce, by appropriate legislation, the provisions of this article.

AMENDMENT XV (1870)

Section 1. The right of citizens of the United States to vote shall not be denied or abridged by the United States or by any State on account of race, color, or previous condition of servitude.

Section 2. The Congress shall have power to enforce this article by appropriate legislation.

AMENDMENT XVI (1913)

The Congress shall have power to lay and collect taxes on incomes, from whatever source derived, without apportionment among the several States, and without regard to any census or enumeration.

AMENDMENT XVII (1913)

The Senate of the United States shall be composed of two Senators from each State, elected by the people thereof, for six years; and each Senator shall have one vote. The electors in each State shall have the qualifications requisite for electors of the most numerous brand of the State legislature.

When vacancies happen in the representation of any State in the Senate, the Executive authority of such State shall issue writs of election to fill such vacancies: Provided, That the legislature of any State may empower the executive thereof to make temporary appointments until the people fill the vacancies by election as the legislature may direct.

This amendment shall not be so construed as to affect the election or term of any Senator chosen before it comes valid as part of the Constitution.

AMENDMENT XVIII (1919)

Section 1. After one year from the ratification of this article, the manufacture, sale, or transportation of intoxicating liquors within, the importation thereof into, or the exportation thereof from the United States and all territory subject to the jurisdiction thereof for beverage purposes is hereby prohibited.

Section 2. The Congress and the several States shall have concurrent power to enforce this article by appropriate legislation.

Section 3. This article shall be inoperative unless it shall have been ratified as an amendment to the Constitution by the legislatures of several States, as provided in the Constitution, within seven years from the date of the submission hereof to the States by the Congress.

AMENDMENT XIX (1920)

The right of citizens of the United States to vote shall not be denied or abridged by the United States or by any State on account of sex.

Congress shall have power to enforce this article by appropriate legislation.

AMENDMENT XX (1933)

Section 1. The terms of President and Vice-President shall end at noon on the 20th day of January, and the terms of Senators and Representatives at noon on the 3rd day of January, of the years in which such terms would have ended; if this article had not been ratified; and the terms of their successors shall then begin.

Section 2. The Congress shall assemble at least once in every year, and such meeting shall begin at noon on the 3rd day of January, unless they shall by law appoint a different day.

Section 3. If, at the time fixed for the beginning of the term of the President, the President elect shall have died, the Vice-President elect shall become President. If a President shall not have been chosen before the time fixed for the beginning of his term, or if the President elect shall have failed to qualify, then the Vice-President elect shall act as President until a President shall have qualified; and the Congress may by law provide for the case wherein neither a President elect nor a Vice-President elect shall have qualified, declaring who shall then act as President, or the manner in which one who is to act shall be selected, and such person shall act accordingly until a President or Vice-President shall have qualified.

Section 4. The Congress may by law provide for the case of the death of any of the persons from whom the House of Representatives may choose a President whenever the right of choice shall have devolved upon them, and for the case of the death of any of the person from whom the Senate may choose a Vice-President whenever the right of choice shall have devolved upon them.

Section 5. Sections 1 and 2 shall take effect on the 15th day of October following the ratification of this article.

Section 6. This article shall be inoperative unless it shall have been ratified as an amendment to the Constitution by the legislatures of three-fourths of the several States within seven years from the date of its submission.

AMENDMENT XXI (1933)

Section 1. The eighteenth article of amendment to the Constitution of the United States is hereby repealed.

Section 2. The transportation or importation into any State, Territory, or possession of the United States for delivery or use therein of intoxicating liquors, in violation of the laws thereof, is hereby prohibited.

Section 3. This article shall be inoperative unless it shall have been ratified as an amendment to the Constitution by conventions in the several States, as provided in the Constitution, within seven years from the date of the submission hereof to the States by the Congress.

AMENDMENT XXII (1951)

Section 1. No person shall be elected to the office of the President more than twice, and no person who has held the office of President, or acted as President, for more than two years of a term to which some other person was elected President shall be elected to the office of the President more than once. But this Article shall not apply to any person holding the office of President when this Article was proposed by the Congress, and shall not prevent any person who may be holding the office of President, or acting as President, during the term within which this Article becomes operative from holding the office of President or acting as President during the remainder of such term.

Section 2. This article shall be inoperative unless it shall have been ratified as an amendment to the Constitution by the legislatures of three-fourths of the several States within seven years from the date of its submission to the States by the Congress.

AMENDMENT XXIII (1961)

Section 1. The District constituting the seat of Government of the United States shall appoint in such manner as the Congress may direct:

A number of electors of President and Vice-President equal to the whole number of Senators and Representatives in Congress to which the District would be entitled if it were a State, but in no event more than the least populous State; they shall be in addition to those appointed by the States, but they shall be considered, for the purposes of the election of President and Vice-President, to be electors appointed by a State; and they shall meet in the District and perform such duties as provided by the twelfth article of amendment.

Section 2. The Congress shall have power to enforce this article by appropriate legislation.

AMENDMENT XXIV (1964)

Section 1. The rights of citizens of the United States to vote in any primary or other election for President or Vice President, for electors for President or Vice president, or for senator or representative in Congress, shall not be denied or abridged by the United States or any state by reason of failure to pay any poll tax or other **tax.**

Section 2. The Congress shall have power to enforce this article by appropriate legislation.

AMENDMENT XXV (1967)

Section 1. In case of the removal of the President from office or of his death or resignation, the Vice President shall become President.

Section 2. Whenever there is a vacancy in the office of Vice President, the President shall nominate a Vice President who shall take office upon confirmation by a majority vote of both Houses of Congress.

Section 3. Whenever the President transmits to the President pro tempore of the Senate and the Speaker of the House of Representatives his written declaration that he is unable to discharge the powers and duties of his office, and until he transmits to them a written declaration to the contrary, such powers and duties shall be discharged by the Vice President as Acting President.

Section 4. Whenever the Vice President and a majority of either the principal officers of the executive departments or of such other body as Congress may by law provide, transmit to the President pro tempore of the Senate and the Speaker of the House of Representatives their written declaration that the President is unable to discharge the powers and duties of his office, the Vice President shall immediately assume the powers and duties of the office as Acting President.

Thereafter, when the President transmits to the President pro tempore of the Senate and the Speaker of the House of Representatives his written declaration that no inability exists, he shall resume the powers and duties of his office unless the Vice President and a majority of either the principal officers of the executive department or of such other body as Congress may by law provide, transmit within four days to the President pro tempore of the Senate and Speaker of the House of Representatives their written declaration that the president is unable to discharge the powers and duties of his office. Thereupon, Congress shall decide the issue, assembling within forty-eight hours for that purpose, if not in session. If the Congress, within twenty-one days after receipt of the latter written declaration, or, if Congress is not in session, within twenty-one days after Congress is required to assemble, determines by two-thirds vote of both Houses that the President is unable to discharge the powers and duties of his office, the Vice President shall continue to discharge the same as Acting President; otherwise, the President shall resume the powers and duties of his office.

AMENDMENT XXVI (1971)

Section 1. The right of citizens of the United States who are eighteen years of age or older to vote shall not be denied or abridged by the United States or by any state on account of age.

Section 2. The Congress shall have power to enforce this article by appropriate legislation.

AMENDMENT XXVII (1992; originally proposed in 1789)

No law, varying the compensation for the services of the Senators and Representatives, shall take effect, until an election of representatives shall have intervened.

Anti-Federalist Writings

The Constitution was submitted for ratification to thirteen states, nine of which had to approve for it to take effect. Anti-Federalists opposed ratification, fearing that the Constitution would establish a strong federal government limiting state and individual freedom. Below are excerpts from selected speeches and writings that reflect some of their views.

George Mason, Speech to the Virginia ratifying convention, 1788

"Mr. Chairman, whether the Constitution be good or bad, the present clause clearly discovers that it is a national government and no longer a confederation. I mean that clause which gives the first hint of the general government laying direct taxes. The assumption of this power of laying direct taxes does, of itself, entirely change the confederation of the states into one consolidated government. This power, being at discretion, unconfined and without any kind of control, must carry everything before it. The very idea of converting what was formerly a confederation to a consolidated government is totally subversive of every principle, which has hitherto governed us.

"This power is calculated to annihilate totally the state governments. Will the people of this great community submit to be individually taxed by two different and distinct powers? Will they suffer themselves to be doubly harassed? These two concurrent powers cannot exist long together; the one will destroy the other: the general government being paramount to and in every respect more powerful than the state governments, the latter must give way to the former. Is it to be supposed that one national government will suit so extensive a country, embracing so many climates and containing inhabitants so very different in manners, habits, and customs?..."

William Findley, Robert Whitehill, and John Smilie, "The Address and Reasons of Dissent of the Minority of the State of Pennsylvania to the Constituents," 1787

"...The powers of Congress under the new Constitution are complete and unlimited over the *purse* and *sword,* and are perfectly independent of and supreme over the state governments, whose intervention in these great points is entirely destroyed. By virtue of their power of taxation, Congress may command the whole or any part of the property of the people. They may impose what imposts upon commerce, they may impose what land taxes, poll taxes, excises, duties on all written instruments and duties on every other article that they may judge proper; in short, every species of taxation, whether of an external or internal nature, is comprised in Article I, Section 8...."

Patrick Henry, Speech to the Virginia ratifying convention, 1788

"...And here I would make this inquiry of those worthy characters who composed a part of the late federal Convention. I am sure they were fully impressed with the necessity of forming a great consolidated government instead of a confederation. That this is a consolidated government is demonstrably clear; and the danger of such a government is, to my mind, very striking. I have the highest veneration for those gentlemen; but, sir, give me leave to demand— What right had they to say, "We, the people"? My political curiosity, exclusive of my anxious solicitude for the public welfare, leads me to ask—Who authorized them to speak the language of "We, the people," instead of "We, the states"? States are the characteristics and the soul of a confederation...."

Richard Henry Lee, Letters from the Federal Farmer to the Republican, October 12, 1787

"...It is to be observed that when the people shall adopt the proposed Constitution it will be their last and supreme act; it will be adopted not by the people of the New Hampshire, Massachusetts, etc., but by the people of the United States; and wherever this Constitution, or any part of it, shall be incompatible with the ancient customs, rights, the laws, or the constitutions heretofore established in the United States, it will entirely abolish them and do them away...."

John Mercer, To the members of the conventions of New York and Virginia, 1788

"...We are persuaded that the people of so large a continent, so different in interests, so distinct in habits, cannot in all cases legislate in one body by themselves or their representatives. By themselves, it is obviously impracticable. By their representatives, it will be found, on investigation, equally so; for if these representatives are to pursue the general interest without constitutional checks and restraints, it must be done by a mutual sacrifice of the interests, wishes, and prejudices of the parts they represent...."

FEDERALIST WRITINGS

In 1787 and 1788 three Federalists (as supporters of the Constitution were called)—James Madison, Alexander Hamilton, and John Jay—advocated ratification of the Constitution with 85 newspaper essays published under the pseudonym Publius. Later these essays were published as *The Federalist Papers*. Below are excerpts from three of the essays.

JAMES MADISON, *Federalist* Number 10

"...(It) may be concluded that a pure democracy, by which I mean a society consisting of a small number of citizens, who assemble and administer the government in person, can admit of no cure for the mischiefs of faction. A common passion or interest will, in almost every case, be felt by a majority of the whole; a communication and concept result from the form of government itself; and there is nothing to check the inducements to sacrifice the weaker party or an obnoxious individual. Hence it is that such democracies have ever been spectacles of turbulence and contention; have ever been found incompatible with personal security or the rights of property; and have in general been as short in their lives as they have been violent in their deaths. Theoretic politicians, who have patronized this species of government, have erroneously supposed that by reducing mankind to a perfect equality in their political rights, they would, at the same time, be perfectly equalized and assimilated in their possessions, their opinions, and their passions.

"A republic, by which I mean a government in which the scheme of representation takes place, opens a different prospect, and promises the cure for which we are seeking. Let us examine the points in which it varies from pure democracy, and we shall comprehend both the nature of the cure and the efficacy, which it must derive from the Union....

"Hence, it clearly appears, that the same advantage, which a republic has over a democracy, in controlling the effects of faction, is enjoyed by a large over a small republic—is enjoyed by the Union over the States composing it. Does the advantage consist in the substitution of representatives whose enlightened views and virtuous sentiments render them superior to local prejudices and to schemes of injustice? It will not be denied that the representation of the Union will be most likely to possess these requisite endowments. Does it consist in the great security afforded by a greater variety of parties, against the event of any one party being able to outnumber and oppress the rest? In an equal degree does the increased variety of parties comprised within the Union increase this security? Does it, in fine, consist in the greater obstacles opposed to the concert and accomplishment of the secret wishes of an unjust and interested majority? Here, again, the extent of the Union gives it the most palpable advantage. The influence of factious leaders may kindle a flame within their particular States, but will be unable to spread a general conflagration through the other States. A religious sect may degenerate into a political faction in a part of the Confederacy; but the variety of sects dispersed over the entire face of it must secure the national councils against any danger from that source. A rage for paper money, for an abolition of debts, for an equal division of property, or for any other improper or wicked project, will be less apt to pervade the whole body of the Union than a particular member of it; in the same proportion as such a malady is more likely to taint a particular county or district, than an entire State...."

ALEXANDER HAMILTON, *Federalist* Number 78

"...A constitution is, in fact, and must be regarded by the judges, as a fundamental law. It therefore belongs to them to ascertain its meaning, as well as the meaning of any particular act proceeding from the legislative body. If there should happen to be an irreconcilable variance between the two, that which has the superior obligation and validity ought, of course, to be preferred; or, in other words, the Constitution ought to be preferred to the statute, the intention of the people to the intention of their agents...."

JOHN JAY, *Federalist* Number 2

"...Providence has been pleased to give this one connected country to one united people—a people descended from the same ancestors, speaking the same language, professing the same religion, attached to the same principles of government, very similar in their manners and customs, and who, by their joint counsels, arms, and efforts, fighting side by side throughout a long and bloody war, have nobly established general liberty and independence.

"This country and this people seem to have been made for each other, and it appears as if it was the design of Providence, that an inheritance so proper and convenient for a band of brethren, united to each other by the strongest ties, should never be split into a number of unsocial, jealous, and alien sovereignties...."

PART FOUR

THE CONSTITUTION AND THE SUPREME COURT

landmark—an object that serves as a guide;
a prominent or distinguishing feature or event

For more than 200 years, Supreme Court decisions have reflected and affected the interpretation of the Constitution. Some decisions have been more important than others in directing the course of the United States. We call these "landmark" decisions.

THE SUPREME COURT

EXAMPLES OF LANDMARK SUPREME COURT DECISIONS

- *Marbury v. Madison* (1803) invalidated a federal law, establishing the Supreme Court's right of judicial review of federal laws to determine their constitutionality.
- *Fletcher v. Peck* (1810) invalidated a state law, establishing the Supreme Court's right of judicial review of state laws to determine their constitutionality.
- *Martin v. Hunter's Lessee* (1816) established the Supreme Court's right of judicial review of state courts' decisions.
- *Dartmouth College v. Woodward* (1819) ruled that private contracts are protected by the Constitution.
- *McCulloch v. Maryland* (1819) asserted the doctrine of implied powers.
- *Cohens v. Virginia* (1821) established supremacy of federal over state law.
- *Gibbons v. Ogden* (1824) asserted a broad interpretation of the commerce clause by ruling that Congress could regulate interstate commerce without interference from the states.
- *Dred Scott v. Sandford* (1857) declared that:
    1) slaves were not citizens; thus Dred Scott, a slave, could not sue in federal courts
    2) Scott's temporary residence in free (Wisconsin) territory did not made him free
    3) the Missouri Compromise of 1820, which prohibited slavery in areas including Wisconsin Territory, was unconstitutional.
- *Plessy v. Ferguson* (1896) validated segregation of white and black races, stating that "separate but equal" facilities were constitutional.
- *Brown v. Board of Education of Topeka* (1954) reversed the 1896 *Plessy* decision on "separate but equal" facilities in regard to education, stating: "Separate educational facilities are inherently unequal."
- *Bush v. Gore* (2000) reversed the 2000 Florida Supreme Court decision on recounting the votes of Palm Beach and Miami-Dade Counties, leaving George W. Bush the winner of Florida's electoral votes. Subsequent to the electoral college vote, Bush became the 43rd president of the United States.

JOHN MARSHALL AND JUDICIAL REVIEW

judicial review—the power of the Supreme Court to declare void all legislative acts contrary to the Constitution

Who shall interpret tthe Constitution and decide whether laws are in agreement with it?

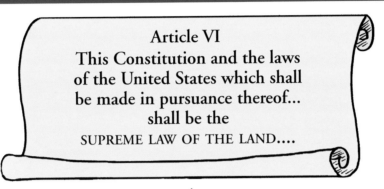

Article VI
This Constitution and the laws
of the United States which shall
be made in pursuance thereof...
shall be the
SUPREME LAW OF THE LAND....

THE PROBLEM:

The Constitution states that it is the supreme law of the land; however, it does not state who shall decide whether a law is in agreement with the Constitution.

FOR EXAMPLE:

What happens if Congress or a state legislature passes a law that seems contrary to the Constitution? Who has the power to review this law and decide whether it is constitutional?

1803—Chief Justice John Marshall claimed the power of JUDICIAL REVIEW for the Supreme Court. Judicial review is the power of the Supreme Court to decide whether a law is constitutional.

JOHN MARSHALL, a Federalist from Virginia, was appointed by John Adams in 1801 to be Chief Justice of the Supreme Court. Marshall was the third Chief Justice—following John Jay and Oliver Ellsworth— and the first to strengthen the Supreme Court.

One of the most outstanding Supreme Court Chief Justices in American history, Marshall dominated the Court during his 34-year term (1801-1835). He wrote most of the opinions himself—including that of *Marbury v. Madison,* which established the principle of judicial review and increased the power of the Court.

It is emphatically the province and duty of the judicial department to say what the law is. [*Marbury v. Madison*]

As Chief Justice, John Marshall strengthened the new government by championing:

1) **NATIONAL SOVEREIGNTY** over states' rights
2) **THE CAPITALIST SYSTEM,** which includes the
   a) right to **private ownership of property**
   b) right to **free enterprise** (work as one chooses)
   c) right to **make a profit.**

He did so through Supreme Court decisions that established these principles:

♦ Broad construction of the Constitution (implied powers)
♦ Broad interpretation of the commerce clause.
♦ Supremacy of federal power over the states and state courts
♦ Freedom of American business from government restraint
♦ Supremacy of capitalism as America's economic system.

His most important decisions include: *Marbury v. Madison, McCulloch v. Maryland,* and *Gibbons v. Ogden.*

MARBURY V. MADISON, 1803—JUDICIAL REVIEW

JOHN ADAMS' "MIDNIGHT APPOINTMENTS"

In 1800 President John Adams, leader of the Federalist party, lost his re-election bid to Thomas Jefferson, leader of the Democratic Republican party.

Just before leaving office, Adams hurridly appointed several Federalist judges to the courts to ensure his party's influence. (Federalists favored national over state power, in contrast to Republicans.)

William Marbury, an Adams appointee, complained about not receiving his commission for justice of the peace of the District of Columbia. But Secretary of State James Madison, whose duty it was to deliver it, ignored the complaint.

This was the first time the Supreme Court declared a law of Congress unconstitutional. It did not do so again until the Dred Scott decision in 1857.

UNDELIVERED MAIL

Adams failed to have all of these commissions delivered before Thomas Jefferson was sworn in as the new president on March 4, 1801.

President Jefferson, angry about what he called Adams' "midnight appointments," told his secretary of state to withhold delivery.

So William Marbury sued for a writ of *mandamus* (a court order forcing a government official to perform the duty of his office), requesting that the **Supreme Court** order Secretary of State James Madison to deliver Marbury's commission.

In 1803 Supreme Court Chief Justice John Marshall dismissed the case. A Federalist appointed by President Adams shortly before he left office, Marshall scolded Madison but ruled against Marbury—for a surprising reason:

The Court ruled that Section 13 of the Judiciary Act of 1789 increasing the Supreme Court's original jurisdiction was <u>unconstitutional</u> because it granted the Court powers not in the Constitution.

JUDICIAL REVIEW

The case *Marbury v. Madison* set forth one of the most important doctrines in our Constitution's history:

> judicial review–the Supreme Court's power to rule on the constitutionality of laws passed by Congress.

Earlier, in the 1798 Kentucky Resolutions, Thomas Jefferson had argued that the power of judicial review belonged to the states.

Now Marshall's ruling made the Supreme Court the **final authority in interpreting the Constitution.**

McCulloch v. Maryland, 1819—Implied Powers

Is the Bank of the U.S. constitutional?

In 1816 Congress chartered the second Bank of the United States (BUS). Some Americans resented this national bank, claiming it catered to the wealthy and gave too much power to the national government.

And besides, many argued, the Constitution did not authorize a national bank, so it must be unconstitutional.

THE BANK IS TOO POWERFUL!

AND I DON'T THINK ITS EVEN CONSTITUTIONAL

Can a state tax a national institution?

State banks, also resentful of the national bank, pressured the Maryland legislature to pass a law taxing all banks not chartered by the state.

The Baltimore branch of the Bank of the United States refused to pay the tax, calling the law unconstitutional.

PAY UP!

WE'LL SEE YOU IN COURT!

State of Maryland

James McCulloch

TAXES DUE

U. S. BANK

The state of Maryland then sued James W. McCulloch, the bank's cashier, for collection of the tax.

McCulloch v. Maryland—the Bank issue

In 1819, with Chief Justice John Marshall presiding, the U. S. Supreme Court heard the case on appeal.

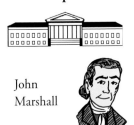

John Marshall

The first question is, has Congress power to incorporate a bank?

Daniel Webster, attorney for the Bank of the United States, responded with a Hamiltonian argument that the Constitution implied this power; therefore, the Bank was constitutional.

Doctrine of implied Powers

John Marshall agreed with Webster's argument that the Bank of the U.S. was constitutional, based on Article I, Section 8 of the Constitution:

Congress shall have power to "...make all laws which shall be necessary and proper for carrying into execution the foregoing powers and all other powers vested by this Constitution in the government of the United States...."

Daniel Webster

WE CAN JUST STRETCH IT A BIT.

CONSTITUTION

This "elastic clause" is called the doctrine of implied powers.

John Marshall cited it in agreeing with Webster and upholding a broad construction of the Constitution.

McCulloch v. Maryland—the Taxation issue

John Marshall

Next, we inquire whether the State of Maryland may, without violating the constitution, tax that branch.

Daniel Webster argued that if the Maryland law were upheld, it would signify state over national supremacy.

NO STATE CAN TAX A FEDERAL INSTITUTION.

Daniel Webster

National supremacy over state power

Chief Justice John Marshall agreed with Webster and struck down as unconstitutional the Maryland law taxing the Bank of the United States.

FOR THE POWER TO TAX IS THE POWER TO DESTROY.

STATE OF MARYLAND

GIBBONS V. OGDEN, 1824—COMMERCE CLAUSE

ROBERT FULTON AND THE CLERMONT

In 1807 Robert Fulton, inventor and artist, designed the first commercially successful steamboat. He named it the *North River Steamboat of Clermont* after the estate of his friend Robert R. Livingston, who had financed the project.

The *Clermont* created a sensation by navigating the Hudson River **upstream** from New York City to Albany (at five miles per hour), a breakthrough in transportation technology.

Aaron Ogden bought an interest in the corporation of Fulton and Livingston and became the successor to the steamboat monopoly they had received from New York state.

WOW — IT'S GREAT TO ENJOY A MONOPOLY IN THIS BUSY AREA.

Aaron Ogden

FULTON AND LIVINGSTON GET A MONOPOLY

In 1808 Fulton and Livingson created a corporation and obtained from the New York legislature a monopoly for operating steamboats on New York waters—including the Hudson River between New York and New Jersey.

MR. FULTON, THIS CHARTER GIVES YOU AND MR. LIVINGSTON EXCLUSIVE RIGHTS TO RUN STEAMBOATS ON THE STATE'S RIVERS.

THANK YOU.

NEW YORK

ROBERT FULTON

Meanwhile, Thomas Gibbons obtained a federal license to run steamboat service in the same area as Ogden, on the Hudson River between New York and New Jersey.

WITH THIS FEDERAL LICENSE, I'LL CONTROL THE STEAMBOAT TRAFFIC BETWEEN NEW YORK AND NEW JERSEY!

U.S. GOVERNMENT

Thomas Gibbons

THE STEAMBOAT CASE

Both Aaron Ogden and Thomas Gibbons claimed the right to steamboat service on the Hudson River. Ogden sued Gibbons to restrain him from trade. The case eventually went to the Supreme Court.

THIS IS MY TERRITORY SO BEAT IT!

OH YEAH? WELL I'VE GOT THE FEDERAL GOVERNMENT ON MY SIDE!

BROAD CONSTRUCTION OF COMMERCE CLAUSE

In 1824 the Supreme Court ruled in favor of Gibbons, invalidating Ogden's New York state monopoly.

Chief Justice John Marshall gave a broad construction to the scope of Congressional power under the commerce clause.

He declared that although states have the power to regulate **intrastate** commerce, the Congressional power to regulate **interstate** and foreign commerce "does not stop at the jurisdictional lines of the several states."

This ruling allowed transportation to develop nationally, free of state restraints.

John Marshall

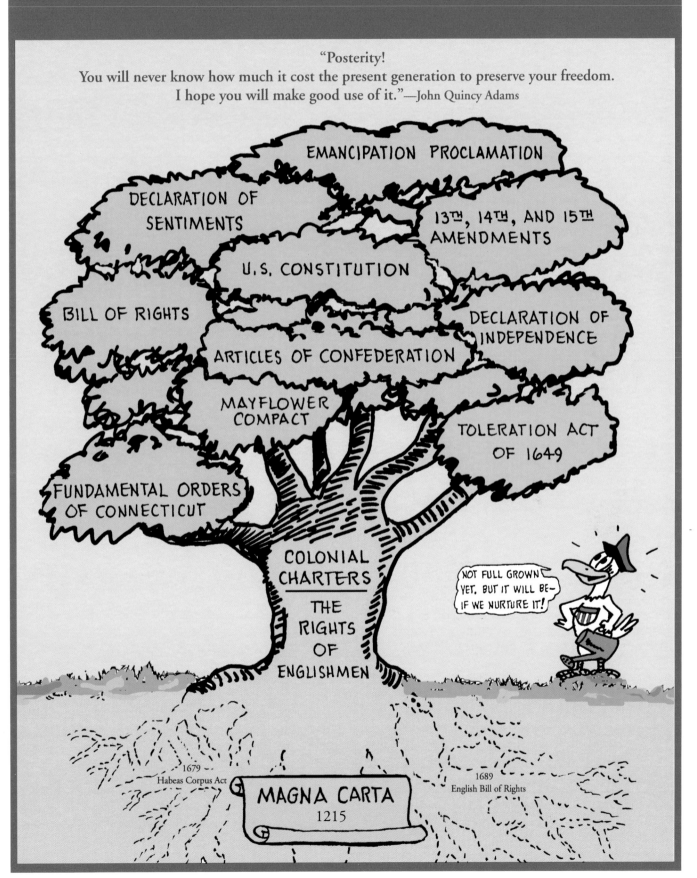

"Posterity!
You will never know how much it cost the present generation to preserve your freedom.
I hope you will make good use of it."—John Quincy Adams

INDEX